Say to This Mountain

The Life of James T. Jeremiah

The Life of James T. Jeremiah

G. K. Belliveau

REGULAR BAPTIST PRESS
1300 North Meacham Road
Schaumburg, Illinois 60173-4806

Dedication
For Patricia

Photo credits (including cover): James T. Jeremiah and Cedarville College

Library of Congress Cataloging-in-Publication Data
Belliveau, G. K. (Gregory Kenneth), 1965–
  Say to this mountain : the life of James T. Jeremiah / G. K. Belliveau.
     p. cm.
  Includes bibliographical references.
  ISBN 0-87227-201-X (pbk.)
  1. Jeremiah, James T.   2. Baptists—United States—Clergy
Biography.   I. Title.
BX6495.J43B45   1999
286'. 1'092—dc21
  [B}   99-20813
                                                                                CIP

SAY TO THIS MOUNTAIN: THE LIFE OF JAMES T. JEREMIAH
© 1999
Regular Baptist Press
Schaumburg, Illinois

Printed in the United States of America
All rights reserved

Contents

Foreword 7

Preface 9

Acknowledgments 11

1   A Tale of Two Cities 13

2   A Thrilling Thing 31

3   A Sound from Heaven 49

4   The Reluctant President 71

5   Raising the Dead 89

6   Your Finest Hour 109

7   Such a Legacy 125

Foreword

A man is truly understood by his loves in life. James T. Jeremiah, foremost, is a lover of his God. Since the day of his salvation, he has dedicated his life to knowing and serving God. Evangelism is his passion (it always has been), for he wants others to know the God Whom he loves so deeply.

This love for God is tied to Jeremiah's love for the Bible. Often we have attended a conference together, and I have found him in the lobby of the hotel reading the Word of God. This commitment to the Truth has translated into a lifetime of godly living.

Dr. Jeremiah loves his family; oh, how he loves his family! God gave him two wonderful helpmeets in Ruby and Ethel, and God gave him super children in Lois, David, Maryalyce, and James. One dare not speak critically of these apples of his eye. He adores his grandchildren and great-grandchildren as well.

His ministry has always centered on his love for the local church and his love of preaching. He loves other preachers, God's people in the congregation, and the hundreds of thousands who have listened to him over the radio for more than fifty years.

One of the major loves of his life has been Cedarville College. He has served her trustees, administrators, faculty, staff, students, alumni, and friends for more than forty-five years as president and chancellor. A rare leader who is a man of strength, conviction, and genuineness, he is one of the most humble men I know. He has never taken himself too seriously or tried to promote himself.

He is one of my dearest friends and most loyal supporters. No president could have a greater encourager as his predecessor.

I love James T. Jeremiah.

PAUL DIXON
President, Cedarville College

Preface

I am a fiction writer, and, as Dickens states in *A Christmas Carol*, "This must be distinctly understood, or nothing wonderful can come of the story I am going to relate." My intention in writing this book was to paint a picture of a life—to piece together vignettes, tales, images, personalities, and places—all the while never losing track of the primary task of every writer: keep the reader turning the page. It is with no apology, therefore, that I state emphatically to my readers that this book is not a *critical* biography but a *narrative* biography. The difference between the two is essential. While the critical biography emphasizes the scholarly aspects (i.e., cross referencing many sources from many angles, from many genres, and from many and various voices), this narrative biography is derived primarily from the subject himself. In other words, this biography should read like a narrative, and my sources are limited to many personal interviews with James T. Jeremiah, snippets from his writings, Ruby Jeremiah's meticulous scrapbooks, and other miscellaneous material. My intention was not to inundate the reader with data, facts, and history; it was to tell a compelling story, to pull the reader into the life of a man and his walk with his God.

My desire was twofold. First, I tried to focus the camera of time on certain elements of James Jeremiah's life, zooming in and panning out in order to show the reader what happens when the God of the universe decides to walk with His faithful. Second, I designed each chapter to emphasize the rapid and almost inconceivable transformation of technology, of culture, and of time, and to juxtapose these elements with the steadfastness of one man and the constancy of Biblical truth.

It is my sincere hope that when the last page is turned, the reader will not only contemplate the life of James T. Jeremiah and the decades in which he lived, but more importantly contemplate his own life and how it relates to the timeless promises of Jesus Christ.

Acknowledgments

I am first and foremost indebted to the kindness and generosity of James T. Jeremiah and his wife, Ethel. Without their help, I never could have written this book. I am in deep gratitude to Dr. Paul Dixon, president of Cedarville College, who allowed me complete and free access to all of the resources and personnel at the college. Also, thanks to Lynn Brock, archivist of Cedarville College Library, for his invaluable services, insights, and detailed bibliographical work; to Carl Brandon for his efforts in videotaping several of my interviews; and to Murray Murdoch for his invaluable sourcebook and personal interviews. I would like to give my warm and heartfelt thanks to close friends John Mortensen and Rick Wolf, whose support and pep talks did more than they could ever imagine. And, finally, thank you to my wife, Patricia, whose encouragement, prayers, and witness make me a better man and a better Christian every day.

Chapter 1

A Tale of Two Cities
(1914–1932)

In 1914 much of the world was beginning to fight World War I, "the war to end all wars." As Europeans sent their sons to the slaughter, the United States waited and watched, self-reliant and seemingly unaware that the heretofore sleeping dogs of violence, economic depression, and human misery would become so ravenous only a few years hence. Indeed, these concerns—political, economic, or otherwise—seemed distant and unobtrusive to Thomas Jeremiah, a gangly farmer living in Corning, a small agricultural community in upstate New York. No, he had more important concerns: his first son, James T. Jeremiah, was about to be born.

Thomas Jeremiah's parents had immigrated to the United States from Wales; he and his brother were the only two children born in this country. His father, settling near Corning, became a farmer, and Thomas picked up the trade, following in the only steps he knew. He acquired more pastureland and still more usable cropland, about 88 acres "up the road and into the valley"[1] south of Corning, along with ten or fifteen milking cows, enough for Thomas to make a living by his hands. The life of a farmer was grueling. He faced long hours behind horse-drawn plows, continual maintenance of equipment, barnyard animals to tend, and the seasonal anxiety of planting, harvesting, and selling the crops. At the turn of the century, electricity and indoor plumbing were for the wealthy; in short, all the amenities taken for granted only forty years later were inconceivable in the early 1900s.

Thomas Jeremiah soon married Flora Rozell, the daughter of "a successful blacksmith and a veteran of the Civil War." She moved up to Corning from Binghamton, New York. Flora's father and mother would become a "real part of my life," recalled James, a hinge pin that would change forever the course of his history.

The faces in the wedding portrait of Thomas and Flora Jeremiah reflect a joyful, happy relationship. Flora wore a long white gown flowing off the picture, her dark hair put up in the fashion of the day, and one of her slim, attractive arms resting playfully on her new husband's shoulder. She was a beautiful woman, elegant, with no obvious apprehension of any tragedies that might lie just around the corner. Thomas, tall and thin, had large, long-fingered hands, one on his knee, the other propped artificially on a dark wooden rest. His face was smooth, with large ears and thinning brown hair neatly combed to the side.

Early in the marriage, Flora became pregnant, but the child died at birth. Several years later she became pregnant again, and on June 11, 1914, James T. Jeremiah came into the world. Five years later, in 1919, she would have another boy, whom they named Edward; and three years after Edward, in 1922, Howard would be born.

Nothing out of the ordinary occurred on that summer day in June, the hot air plastering the dirt-stained shirt to Thomas's back, as the cries from the newborn James echoed through the bedroom and out into the windswept acres beyond. No birth was considered easy in the beginning of the twentieth century; the infant mortality rate was still high, especially in rural communities. The world was rumbling with rumors of a great and hideous war; but on that summer day in June, life and exuberance issued from

A Tale of Two Cities

the tiny mouth of little James and through the warm, caressing eyes of Flora Jeremiah.

* * *

Although life on the farm was filled with chores—drawing water for the day; cutting, gathering, and stacking firewood for the wood-burning stove; helping Thomas in the fields—the three boys were able to find time to chase each other, wrestle, and make mischief as young boys do. Later in his life James would recall, "We had a place for the cows, a pasture field with a big swamp. The cows loved it because it had a lot of grass around it. Someone asked me one day why I don't play golf. Well, I said, 'When I was a kid, I made a practice of chasing white cows all over the pasture, and I'll be hanged if I will waste my time on a little white ball.'"

The Jeremiah farm bordered a fruit farm on one side and another large field on the other. Both adjacent properties had working distilleries for making whiskey. The fruit farmer would routinely take the distillery into his house and put it on the front burner of his stove. "We would have dinner with him and his family on occasion, and that still would be working in the background. One day we [James and his father] were out in the woods, and we found two kegs of whiskey. I tried to get my father to shoot a hole in them, but he wouldn't do it."

In the age of horse-drawn carts, travel was tedious, smelly, and long. Flora would regularly gather the three boys, put them in the wagon, and journey four miles to town. James would sit with Howard and Edward, listening to the creaking of the wheels, the whipping of the horse's tail, the clip-clop of the hooves rhythmically pounding the dirt road.

On special occasions in the summertime, when the August heat beat down upon the countryside, Flora would buy ice-cream cones for her sons. And on the return trip, it was Edward who took his time, licking the drips slowly, intentionally. James and Howard, consumed with the smooth, sweet, delicious treat, slurped and licked their cones to a soggy nub. And as the ice cream dripped down their hands and chins, drying to a sticky film in the humid air, Edward, still patiently licking and silently watching his brothers, smiled with delight. The long trip home soon became unbearable, the small wagon filled with the sounds of loud, deliberately provocative chides toward the middle brother still enjoying his slowly melting, carefully licked ice-cream cone.

The town of Corning was a hub for James' father as well. Thomas worked the fields in the spring and summer. Then in the empty winter months, he would daily walk four miles in all sorts of weather to catch a trolley that would take him to the Corning Glass Works. It was this Welsh tenacity and stubbornness in James that God would first strip and then use for His glory.

While Howard stayed with Flora, James and Edward would walk three miles each day to a one-room schoolhouse. The trip, as could be imagined, was long, arduous, and—for a child uninterested in academics—"hard to go: a terrible ten miles there and three to come home." But there in a tiny building that included all eight grades and thirty students, James would learn his "3 *R*'s," be introduced to his first educational experiences, and soon become familiar with the ropes of institutional learning. He would recall later in his life that "the teachers were always kind, always tried to help, but did not put up with any nonsense. They knew what it was to practice the laying on of hands. They had other ways to make you listen as well."

The years passed with little change to the Jeremiah family. The "Great War" had ended, its battle scars severe but healing. Several years down the road would come the second terrible blow to the age of infinite progress: the financial crash of 1929. That economic free fall paved the way for a depression that would tear once again into America's economic and social fabric. But the Jeremiah family, like others during the early part of the century, could not foresee such hardships, for they were engrossed in the business of living. Soon they would have a wake-up call that would leave them reeling.

Certain events in our histories move us or sweep us toward our destiny. They are turning points ordained by a sovereign God to bring us to Himself. The Bible is replete with individuals in such situations. Joseph was sold into slavery, accused by Potiphar's wife, and put into prison, only to reign over all of Egypt as Pharaoh's number-two man. Jesus, the ultimate paradox of bad things happening to good people (indeed in His case, a perfect and sinless person), was nailed to a cross unjustly before His accusers. Yet through such divine action, the world received access to the throne of grace, and sins could be washed away by the blood of that spotless Lamb. Throughout all of history, God has been working His divine will in those who will acknowledge it, those who will surrender themselves to Omnipotence. For some, such a blow, such a hit by the hammer of God, is cursed. For others, however, it is a life-changing renewal and a step closer to a holy and loving God. The year 1926 was that time for Thomas, Flora, James, Edward, and little Howard Jeremiah.

It was a cold winter, and snow had covered all of the pasture. Bits of brown weeds, stiff and straw-like, pushed up through the drifts of snow; others folded over, hollowing out shelters for whatever fortunate animal could find it. It was mid-afternoon, and twelve-year-old James rode with his father out to the woods to cut and gather firewood for the night ahead. The crunch of the horse's hooves across the thin frozen crust was mingled with the animal's heavy breathing, snorts of steam exploding from its nostrils and mouth. The two men made their way through several drifts, across the fields, and into the outer edge of the woods. James and his father spent the afternoon gathering, cutting, stripping, and piling up a surplus of kindling and logs.

One could imagine the scene: the cows foraging around in the nearby pastures and lowing as they move from one grazing spot to the next. Perhaps a wind rocks the bare trees and creaks their long branches. Then suddenly, above the sounds, James makes out a shrill voice. He continues to stack and gather, but again is pulled to a stop by the shrill calls. Thomas, noticing his son, also stops to listen; the voice in the distance is alarmed, filled with hysteria. Something is wrong.

From over the hill, trudging through the snow, falling down, rising again out of the large drifts, Edward comes, screaming. What he says is unintelligible, but his meaning is quite clear: *emergency!* It is a cry for help. Thomas throws down his ax and strides toward the panic-stricken boy. As Edward comes closer, the message hits like terrible fists.

"Howard is sick! He is very sick! You better get down there!"

That four-year-old Howard was sick was not news to James and his father, for he had been down with a fever for several days. But the panic in Edward's voice and the fact that the boy had run to get them quickly commanded their attention.

James and Edward jumped into the back of the sleigh, while their father whipped the horse into a lope. The cold breeze stung James' cheek. A fear gripped them all. When they entered the house, there lay Howard, unconscious, his breath garbled and wheezing. Thomas quickly called for the doctor, harnessed the horse to the sleigh, and rode to Corning to fetch him. The doctor arrived and examined the sickly boy: high fever, headache, diarrhea, and, there on his stomach, the all too familiar rose-colored spots. Howard had typhoid fever. The fever had rapidly progressed into bronchitis, and the doctor feared pneumonia. The entire house was at risk, and since the symptoms occur one to three weeks after infection, other members of the family could already have been infected.[2]

Typhoid fever is caused by unsanitary living conditions. This type of outbreak, which took so many lives at the turn of the century, rouses people little today. Most rural areas, even decades after the 1920s, had no indoor plumbing. Drinking water obtained from the well outside had to be carried into the house in buckets to be heated for cooking, cleaning, and washing. Only city dwellers had modern-day bathrooms. The majority of Americans used outhouses, wooden shacks built over deep holes. These holes would drain into cesspools located somewhere close by. After the holes filled, the outhouse was moved to a new location, the old hole buried. Since the well was usually located quite near the outhouse or the cesspool, the potential for contamination of drinking water and food was extremely high. Further, a farmer working in the barn with the animals would track bacteria into the house, which could easily infect the entire family.

That night James did not sleep. He lay awake listening to his younger brother struggling for breath, the raspy inhalations, the sputtering of phlegm, the desperate battle for life. That sound, that personal experience with death, would haunt him the rest of his life. Several days later, little Howard died. The family was devastated. James would admit seventy years later that "the sorrow of Howard's death is still a part of my life, as I think of that little boy going through all of that. I am sure he went to Heaven, because I am sure God takes care of babies."

But it was Flora, James' mother, who was hit the hardest. "She was brokenhearted. She loved that boy. She loved all of us, and she loved him. She didn't want to see him go."

She who had already lost one child at birth was especially close to Howard, for he was the baby, the one with her during the day while Thomas worked in the fields and James and Edward went to school. One can only imagine the loss from such a blow. But her grief was soon squelched by the tyranny of the urgent.

The doctor's diagnosis had been correct, for just after Howard's death, James' brother Edward showed symptoms of typhoid fever. Flora was determined not to lose another son, so they took him to Thomas's brother downtown. James Jeremiah (the very uncle James T. was named after) was a successful tinsmith who worked on roofs and furnaces in Corning. Moving Edward to Corning removed him from the contamination, but more trouble was to follow. Thomas suddenly showed signs of fever and became weak, the red blotches appearing on his stomach. He, too, had typhoid fever. Flora was desperate. She called the doctor, who told her to take him to the hospital. The carriers of the bacteria had to be identified and controlled, or further death would result. In those days taking someone to the hospital was rare and was considered an act of desperation. A rural farmer did not have the resources to pick up and leave his home to have a family member cared for in an institution. Illness, births, and even deaths were common occurrences within the home during the early decades of the twentieth century. Taking Thomas to the hospital in Corning was the action of a fearful wife who believed that her family was on the brink of oblivion.

The walls of security had suddenly crashed in ruin around the Jeremiah family. While James' father was treated at the hospital, James' brother was recovering in Corning. Then it became apparent that James himself was infected with something: the measles. Now that she and James were the only ones at the farm, Flora, emotionally and physically drained, could focus all of her attention on her oldest son.

She "had a hard time of it," but persevered; for "she had a real love for her family, a love for the boys, a real concern."

While Thomas and Edward recovered from their illness, young James, man of the house at twelve years old, would have to keep the farm running. But this responsibility was too much for an inexperienced youth. "I had tried to operate the farm, take care of the cows. I never did learn how to milk. Couldn't do it then and can't do it to this day." The daily routine soon grew to be a monumental burden for Flora and James. After returning from the hospital, James' father soon made an effort to help out as he could. Weak from his illness, he would still go out and lend a hand in the fields. While James guided the plow through the dark soil, Thomas would walk alongside and "sort of drive the horses." After they had reached the end of the furrow, James and his father would lift the plow, turn it around, and then head back the other way.

The Corning farm was too much for James and his father to manage. That was about the time that Edward Rozell, James' grandfather, called from Johnson City. The farm was deteriorating rapidly, and Rozell knew that his daughter and son-in-law needed help. He issued an invitation, and it wasn't long until the couple accepted. James' father and mother packed up essential items and shipped them to Johnson City by train, taking little else with them on the eighty-mile journey to their new home. The house they left behind was overrun and ravished with the haunting memories of little Howard's death and the terrible battle with typhoid. It was time to move out, move away, start fresh with familiar people. The hand of God had suddenly gripped the family and pushed them in a new direction.

Edward Stanley Rozell, James' grandfather, had seen great changes in the country. Indeed, after his father's death in the Civil War, he quickly enlisted, but was barely taken because he was legally too young to join with the North. James would recall, "When I was pastor in Dayton, a lady in the congregation had a sister visiting from North Carolina. She introduced me to the sister, and her sister said, 'My grandfather fought in the Civil War.'

"I said, 'So did mine.' She could tell by my accent that it wasn't on the same side, and she was ready to fight it all over again."

When the bloody Civil War ended, Edward Rozell married Mary Jane Brown and became a successful blacksmith outside Johnson City. By the time the Jeremiah family moved in, Mr. Rozell was retired and was living well in a comfortable house. Thick in the shoulders with strong hands from his life at the anvil and hammer, Edward Rozell had become quite a distinguished gentlemen. His wife, Mary Jane, was a plump woman who, so characteristic of family portraits of that time, looked sullen wearing a dark cumbersome Victorian dress, hair up, wire spectacles masking saddened eyes.

James and his family soon settled into a routine at 134 Ackley Avenue. The house had plenty of space for them to shake off the cares from Corning and begin the business of living once again. "We had four bedrooms, room enough for all of us. My mother and father had the front room. My brother Edward and I had the side room."

James' father was soon hired at the 1900 Washer Company. By this time he had regained his old self. "He was an interesting fellow, you know. He smoked cigarettes and a pipe. But if he had ever caught us smoking, he would have paddled the life out of us. When he got typhoid fever, he lost the appetite for tobacco; but when he got better, he went back to it." His father also experimented with homemade beer. "I tasted that once," James would later note with a grimace. "Thank the Lord it cured me from ever becoming a drunk. It was abominable!" Thomas presently landed a job as a janitor at the local high school, and eventually he became the superintendent of janitorial services for five schools in the district. The changes that would occur in his spiritual life would be minimal. He had been prompted by God to share in a new life, but he decided instead to grind out his future on his own.

Flora Jeremiah took a job in the office of the Endicott Johnson Corporation, a shoe factory. When the Depression ravished the United States, James' mother was thus able to help provide needed care and provisions for the family. "They [the Endicott Johnson Corporation] took care of their workers. They had health service for them and everything. Although the Depression was real and you could feel it, we didn't lose anything through it. We had enough to eat. The Lord took care of us. We were never really hungry."

James' grandparents were Christian, God-fearing people who prayed before every meal and at the close of each day. Before James would fall asleep, he would hear his grandparents pray. "That made an impression on me. They prayed out loud. I didn't know what they prayed, brother, but they were talking to the Lord. That made an impression on me for all of my life."

James, Flora, Edward, and the grandparents regularly attended a Methodist church in Binghamton, which was a far cry from the lack of spiritual nourishment James had received in Corning. "I went to a church [when living in Corning] with a neighbor, but I look back upon it now and am glad I didn't go there regularly: there was not enough gospel to get saved." James' mother, unable to attend church in Corning due to distance and the fact that her husband lacked interest in Christianity, jumped at the chance in Johnson City. She would take the two boys to church when she could and played the violin for the church orchestra. James would recall years later the power that the church had on his life. "I remember revival meetings and hearing the gospel. I got under conviction. I didn't get saved then. That old boy [the preacher] had a message to tell the people about getting saved. I don't know what the church is today. They probably don't even know how to spell the word 'saved.' That thing [the church] is about as gone as a gone goose."

In one of God's little ironies, James was able to obtain a job peddling papers throughout the neighborhood. On his route he would stop at the Practical Bible Training School. "I went into the office one day to peddle papers, and John A. Davis, the president, was on the telephone. He looked at me sternly and said, 'Be quiet!'" And James stood stiff, dramatically holding out a paper as though he were a statue. He would later remember a time when several of the school's solicitors came knocking at his grandfather's door looking for financial support. James asked his grandfather why he wouldn't contribute. "Well," Edward Rozell answered, "I told them that I shoed John Davis's horses for the wagons, and when he pays me the money that he owes me for that, then I'll give something."

"But they were kind to me. Mrs. Davis particularly, the wife of the founder of the school, was a fine woman and a real testimony to me as an unsaved boy." The seminary that James would later attend would be an offshoot of that very institution.

One of the biggest changes that occurred in James' life during this time was his schooling. The new facility was a large city school, a far cry from the one-room school that he had attended in Corning. When James first entered the immense brick building and saw the many classrooms filled with hundreds of children, he "nearly died of fright. This old country boy didn't know what to do." Although a shock at the time, this step into the life of the city, its people, and the ways of the world was preparing him for the road that lay before him.

James was not a good student, and like most kids his

age he wanted to be done with academics as soon and as painlessly as possible. He hated the class oral English (speech class), and tried to duck out of it as much as possible, little realizing that his ministry would someday be made from the very skills taught in that class.

One day he was sitting in another despised class, biology. He was acting up, for he did not care for the teacher and cared even less for the evolutionary theory that she was teaching. Even then in his unregenerate days, James did not like being traced back to a monkey. He was told to sit up, stay in his seat, and quit fidgeting. He continued to be a nuisance. She warned him again, and he refused. Finally the instructor, frustrated and out of patience, walked over to him and sternly commanded, "James, you sit up there, or I will send you to your father." Then as now, "it is a very unsatisfactory arrangement to be a student where your father is the custodian or teacher." James straightened up, for the fear of his father's wrath settled upon his antsy limbs. When he got home, he told his father what had happened. "What would you have done if she had sent me to you?" he asked.

Thomas sucked on his pipe for a moment and then blew out a stream of smoke. "I'd send you back to her and tell her that if she couldn't take care of you, I don't know who could." These are the types of words a young rambunctious teen wishes to hear, and probably they spell doom for a biology teacher.

It was during those high school days that James was truly confronted with the gospel. One day while he was over at the house of his friend Edgar Erieg, a man came to the door.

"Edgar, you haven't been to Sunday School lately. You should come. We have a fine class, a good basketball team." That was all it took: basketball. James told Edgar after the man had left, "You and I are going to Sunday School next week."

That next week they did go, played basketball at the church, and listened to the Sunday School teacher, who, no matter what the topic was, ended the message with Jesus' dying on the cross and an exhortation: "You boys need the Lord."

James listened but did not respond. He was in those years of "immortality," the teen years where life is forever and health and well-being are part of the package. Yet the tragedy of losing his brother and that feeling of emptiness and loss were perhaps beginning to catch up with him.

Then tragedy struck the Jeremiah family again in 1932, James' junior year in high school. As the family gathered for dinner, James' grandfather bowed his head and asked God's blessing on the food. The family began to eat as usual. James would recall the rest years later:

> I know that we were sitting at the table. Franklin D. Roosevelt was running for office, and the radio was on. My father, after he had finished his dinner, went to listen. All of the sudden my grandfather slumped forward. Dad and I carried him to the front room and laid him on the davenport, but he was dead.

The man who had brought Christ into the Jeremiah household, the man who had for so long been a kind, considerate guide and mentor to young James, a man who had seen the worst and the best in the world died peacefully at the respectable age of eighty-three. It would be James' second experience with death, an experience that would press itself deep into his soul.

One particular day the Sunday School teacher pulled James aside.

"I want you to do something for me."

"What?" James responded with an indifferent shrug.

"I want you to read the Gospel of John and ask the Lord to show you the truth."

James paused and shrugged again, but agreed. That night he opened the Gospel of John:

A Tale of Two Cities

> In the beginning was the Word, and the Word was with God, and the Word was God.... All things were made by him; and without him was not any thing made that was made. In him was life; and the life was the light of men. And the light shineth in darkness; and the darkness comprehended it not.

He read the entire book of John and through that experience was converted. "I can't tell you the date, though I can tell you the place: it was at home. I don't know all the details of it, but I know the Lord saved me. It used to bother me that I could not tell the date or the hour and so on. But then I remembered that salvation is a new birth. I had already had one birth, and I couldn't remember that; so why should I have to remember the other one?"

That he was saved relatively later in his youth would drive James' subsequent strong feelings on Christian education and the need for a vibrant youth program.

> Suppose that Paul had been converted at seventy instead of twenty-five. There would be no Paul in history. There was a Matthew Henry because he was converted at eleven and not at seventy; a Dr. Isaac Watts because he was converted at nine and not at ninety; a Jonathan Edwards because he was converted at eight and not eighty; a Richard Baxter because he was converted at six and not at sixty. If our young people are not reached for Christ when they are young, they are likely not to be won to Him at all.[3]

Soon after graduation in 1933, at nineteen, James sought employment in Endicott. He was just beginning to feel the gnawing of the Holy Spirit that would eventually drive him headlong into the ministry. But James, at that time not heeding the call, decided to take the trolley into town to find a job. The family still did not have an automobile; in fact, it would not be until both James and Edward had moved out of the house that their parents would finally get a Ford—one for Thomas and one for Flora.

IBM was a fledgling company at the time, and James got a job working on punch clocks or time card clocks. His job was to test to see that the clock was functioning and that the time registered correctly upon the card. The work was dull and monotonous, eight hours of drudgery. James was beginning to feel the definite call of God upon his life, yet from that earlier time when he had delivered newspapers to the Practical Bible Training School, he had an overwhelming dread of having to preach. Somehow, even before his salvation, he had sensed that God desired him to preach the gospel.

Finally, the feeling of conviction was so great that James decided he had to do something about it. After much consideration, he knew he had to get more Bible training. Baptist Bible Seminary, an offshoot from the place where he had delivered papers as a youth, would become his first stepping-stone into a life of full-time ministry.

"One day I felt the Lord calling me to preach," James would reminisce. "I had to do something. So I went to Tommy Flynn, my boss who was a Catholic, and said, 'Tommy, I am going to quit. I am going to seminary to become a pastor.' And I will never forget his response. He said, 'Jimmy, that is a great thing to do. You will never regret doing that. I am so glad you are doing that.' "

Tommy wasn't necessarily glad that James was quitting, for James was a good worker; but even Tommy must have sensed the Lord's working in this young man's life and felt the need to encourage him. And that was one of the first confirmations to James as he tested out his new wings of faith. God was moving, and now he needed to be obedient. God had done so much in saving a rambunctious, prideful young man. And now James was ready to begin to be used, to go where he could be most effective. Little did he know that the great mountains before him would dwarf Mount

Everest in comparison. It is in the little things, in the present, not yesterday or tomorrow, that God builds character and tenacity. The seminary would be James' first real step of obedience toward a lifetime of Christian service.

ENDNOTES
1. All quotations of James T. Jeremiah, unless otherwise noted, are from personal interviews conducted by the author.
2. *Guidelines for the Control of Infectious Diseases: Typhoid and Paratyphoid Fevers*. Online. Internet. 22 June 1998. Available: http://hna.ffh.vic.gov.au/phb/hprot/inf_dis/bluebook/typoid.htm
3. James T. Jeremiah, *The House That Stands* (Cedarville, Ohio: Christian Educational Publication, 1976), 30.

Chapter 2

A Thrilling Thing
(1933–1939)

"Mr. Jeremiah," demanded E. H. Bancroft, a revered but intimidating instructor at Baptist Bible Seminary. Bancroft was of medium build, balding, with a sweep of white hair jutting out across his scalp. His overly thick glasses created the illusion of bulbous eyes, eyes which in effect were nearly useless—he was all but blind.[1] "Mr. Jeremiah, quote for us the key verses in Romans where Paul explains, . . ." he paused for a moment, glasses gleaming in the dim light of the church classroom, ". . . God's sovereignty and how it affects man."

James was now a tall, lanky young man of twenty with long wavy hair brushed straight back, looking as though at any moment it would spring up into a shrub of wiry chaos. The class was Bancroft's notorious systematic theology. James shifted in his seat and then responded with much faltering. He finished, and there was a long pause.

Bancroft peered around the room at the blurs surrounding him. "Well, class," he added, smiling sardonically, "that is the Jeremiah version. Now we will have the Authorized Version." And without any hesitation, E. H. Bancroft quoted the appropriate verses. "He could," James would recall, "quote it, or almost any other verse you would ask, from memory."

Baptist Bible Seminary, founded one year before James Jeremiah became a Christian, was, according to him, "built for me, brother." The seminary was an offshoot of Practical Bible Training School. Richard Murphy and Dr. A. A. Wright, as well as other disgruntled faculty members, had become "sick and tired of what was going on there [PBTS] . . . so they didn't make a fuss, they just left" and began BBS. Murphy pastored the First Baptist Church, a large and prominent institution in Johnson City, New York; so, using that building as their base, the twelve faculty and staff members began expounding and teaching the Word of God. These men and women would lay the foundation for James' life of ministry.

The seminary was close by, about three miles away, and James would walk there from his grandparents' house at 134 Ackley Avenue. The death of Edward Rozell, James' grandfather, had been a shock to the family, but life rolled on with its busyness. Edward, James' brother, was just starting high school, and James' father and mother were both working in the city. Thomas and Flora Jeremiah did not say much when James told them about his plans for ministry. They were concerned with his leaving a good job at IBM and "preferred that I get a job and make money, but they never criticized me about going."

It is always hard for an unbelieving family to grasp the urgency and hunger that springs forth out of the heart and soul of a newly converted child of God. Thomas Jeremiah must have felt some pride, or at least curiosity, in his son's newly acquired interest. For during James' stint in seminary, he would on various Sunday mornings harness his horse and wagon and drive his son to his preaching engagement. Thomas would chauffeur his son to each church, sit patiently through the service, and then drive him home.

"Son," his father said one beautiful day while staring straight ahead and flicking the reins to keep the horses in line, "if you are going to be a preacher, then you have got to speak louder." And that was that. The oral English class, so dreaded in high school, had been brought back to life by a most unlikely source.

It is hard for any biographer to reconstruct a life, to bring to the reader a rich sense of time and place, to paint a full and complete life from scant and sometimes unreliable sources. But from the data gathered, it appears that James had a unique and meaningful time at the Baptist Bible Seminary.

Out of the eleven faculty members at the seminary, five would have a lasting impression on James: President Harold Commons, E. H. Bancroft, A. A. Wright, Mabel Thomson, and Hazel Vibbard.

Miss Mabel Thomson was a former Presbyterian. Stiff and dignified, she had a rich Calvinistic heritage, a heritage with little room for humor. She taught several classes: Bible history, church history, Biblical criticism, and Public Speaking II and III. James would remember later her sage advice during speech class: "You fellows go out to preach. And so that your knees don't shake, you had better get down on them." Her patience was notoriously short for antics of any kind, and the case with Hiawatha was no different.

One day during speech class, Bob Hayden, a short-haired young man with a receding hairline, a person who "loved the Lord and eventually became a pastor out on Long Island," was standing next to James just as class was about to begin. Miss Thomson walked up to Bob with a stern look on her face, for he was wearing a large sign with the word *Hiawatha* across its front. There were to be no shenanigans in her class, so she calmly looked at the young man and inquired, "Hiawatha, Mr. Hayden?" Which elicited from Bob a loud and obnoxious: "Hi-'a, paleface!" And without cracking a smile, Miss Thomson began lecturing the class on the day's lesson.

In addition to being serious about their classes, such as Dr. Bancroft's and Miss Thomson's, BBS students were serious about Christian service and outreach. Christian Endeavor, a service-based gathering for boys and girls, would meet during the evenings. There were two levels: senior and intermediate. One of James' classmates described the typical meeting:

> They are lustily singing one of their favorite choruses, "Follow Jesus." One of the most important phases of their work is Scripture memorization. As the roll is called, each member present answers with a verse from the Word. It thrills us to hear these boys and girls lead in prayer, thanking God for His blessings and seeking wisdom and direction for their lives. One of the seminary students will present the lesson for the evening.

But in such a spiritual atmosphere, there was always room for levity. In a section of James' 1935 yearbook titled "Jokes," several humorous incidents that took place during the academic year are recorded.[2] While most of them are corny, and like all inside jokes are relevant only for those involved with the actual event, several of the anecdotes paint a picture of comradery, affection, and fun:

> James Jeremiah: Can you give one good reason for being single?
>
> D. Santmier: Yes, I was born that way.
>
> * * *
>
> Professor Bancroft (systematic theology): Will the draft from that open window blow on any of you young ladies?
>
> Mr. Teachout: No, it's quite all right, thank you.
>
> Professor Bancroft: I was speaking to the ladies, not the ladies' man!
>
> * * *

A Thrilling Thing

>Miss Dunleavy (elemental theology): Can you quote a passage to substantiate your point, Mr. Reed?
>
>Mr. Reed: (without giving reference): "Ye are of your father the Devil."
>
>Professor Bancroft: Who are you speaking to?
>
>* * *
>
>Juniors were contending for the possession of a classroom. Miss Vibbard arrived for her class.
>
>Mr. Houser (junior): How about a game of marbles [winner gets the room]?
>
>Miss Vibbard: No, how about checkers, and it's your move?

In 1935 James was a junior at the seminary. In his school picture, he was a thick-haired, tall, thin boy dressed in a sweater and a tie, standing in the back row. Standing in the row before him was his close friend Clara Crumb, a round-faced, happy young woman. And in the front row, hands folded across her waist, curly hair combed to the side, stood his future wife, Ruby Lathrop. In a class of only eleven students, lasting friendships and soul mates were easy to come by. That year, however, neither James nor Ruby was aware that the other would be his or her future life partner. No, there was systematic theology, public speaking, and homiletics to survive and basketball in the fall. James did not even consider Ruby at that time, for he was dating someone else, whom he thought he would marry.

Since basketball had been a vehicle in his conversion to Christ, James immediately became involved with the Baptist Bible Seminary team. During his junior year he was elected business manager, and along with the team captain, "led the team through strenuous games and practices, . . .

secured contests, and made all necessary arrangements for their being carried out."³ In the team picture of 1935, James is seated on the end, broad shouldered—wavy head of hair greased back, emphasizing his long forehead—socks rolled down to the top of his sneakers, a young man vigorous for competition and the love of sport.

Practices were held every Tuesday and Thursday, and since the team was small and not part of any college associations, the team members were in charge of setting up their own games. They would travel to neighboring towns to compete, "while the greater share were played at home in the gymnasium of the church."⁴ A key to just how small the team was and how diligent each player had to be to play is found in the 1935 *Seminarion:* "The hours spent in practicing as well as those spent in actual contests proved a welcome recreation, *enough players being present nearly every practice period to form two opposing teams*" [italics added].⁵

In 1935, far from the small seminary, the cauldron of war was beginning to simmer. On March 8, Hitler revealed that he had an air force and that he was eager to execute all branches of his military. By March 16, Germany had denounced the Treaty of Versailles and reintroduced universal military conscription. By September the Nuremberg Laws were implemented, abolishing the rights of all Jews. Hitler's long arm reached even to the German Protestant churches, placing them under state control.⁶

The year 1936 would be a milestone in James Jeremiah's walk with God. It was also the continuation of the crisis in Europe. Joseph Stalin had begun "The Great Purge." By 1938 more than ten million people would be dead because of it. And on March 7, Germany moved into the demilitarized zone in the Rhineland.⁷ But these issues were far from the mind of a young man who was entering his last year of seminary and who had now found himself head over heels in love.

A Thrilling Thing

James' friendship with Ruby Lathrop began during their first official class officer meeting. He had been nominated president of his graduating class, and Ruby was vice president. James had broken up with a young woman whom he had thought was "a good one" for marriage. He had then withdrawn from romantic pursuits, trusting in God to fulfill his needs. It must have taken a lot of courage for James to allow his heart to be placed on the block as he did, for years later he would recall that he was "hesitant for a long time" to start the dating process again.

Anyone who has been involved with a small college or high school knows how difficult intimate relationships are to forge and then to cut asunder and how difficult it is to remain on a Christ-centered plane, not allowing envy, jealousy, or gossip to sprout and mature into rancorous weeds. In a school of sixty students, and in a senior class of only ten—most at that age wanting to find mates and vocations before leaving to serve Christ—the ground would appear fertile for such ungodly growth. Yet these negative emotions, though probably present at the time, soon dissipated on all fronts. Concerning his former girlfriend, James remarks, "We remained friends all our lives. . . . When her husband died, Ruby and I went up to see her." Here is the mark of a true Christian: the spirit of love and forgiveness, where friendship is bound not by carnal or worldly attitudes but by the Holy Spirit, the Word of God, and a commitment to serve Christ no matter what.

The academic year progressed, along with James and Ruby's relationship. Ruby had gone to Baptist Bible Seminary from Springville, Pennsylvania. She was studying to receive her diploma in Christian service. At that time the seminary (later to become Baptist Bible College) did not grant degrees, but certificates stating that the student had accomplished all the objectives for his or her specific field. It was a place to learn the foundational skills needed to go on to further education or to become involved directly in full-time ministry. One of Ruby's three brothers, Clifford, a spectacled, bow-tied, scholarly looking young man, graduated one year before she did. It appears from the *Seminarion* that Clifford and Ruby both arrived at Baptist Bible Seminary in 1935, James Jeremiah's junior year.[8]

Both Ruby and James graduated in 1936; the 1935 yearbook explains the fevered pitch that all graduating seniors must have experienced:

> THESES are due! Everywhere a frantic search. Theologies were consulted, libraries were packed to the doors with students and as the time for completion drew near one could hear the scratch, scratching anywhere as fountain pens rewrote Dr. Bancroft's theology.[9]

This fevered pitch was followed by a "post examination recuperation party. Juniors entertaining."[10] And as the year wound down, James and his graduating class would fill their days finishing up homiletics, editing the *Seminarion*, preparing for final exams, and writing graduation messages.[11]

When James and Ruby were engaged, they decided "not to get married until the Lord opened the door of service." The academic year came to a close, but still there was no word concerning James' future in ministry. God seemed silent. It was their good friend and classmate Clara Crumb who would be the messenger of long-awaited glad tidings. Clara had grown up in western New York, in Niobe, a small town two miles outside Panama, where she attended church. She knew that her church was looking for a pastor, and she suggested James. Soon after that, the deacons asked James to be a guest preacher, to go down and fellowship, talk, get to know each other, and help the congregation decide if he were the right person to fill the position.

James did not own or have access to a car at the time, so

A Thrilling Thing

he took a train to Jamestown, New York, and one of the congregation picked him up at the depot. He preached several messages in Panama, and each time he felt a stronger and stronger conviction in his heart that the Panama church was his first calling as a pastor. Indeed, it wasn't long until the church did invite James to be pastor. God had answered his prayer, and by doing so had given His blessing upon James and Ruby's marriage compact. This incident would become just one more example in James' life of instances in which God specifically answered the cries of an earnest saint.

James and Ruby graduated in June 1936 and were married October 1 of the same year. The trees had turned a rusty brown and red, and some tinges of yellow still persisted as the winter months fast approached. The wedding was to be held in Springville at Ruby's parents' house. James had borrowed a car from the church custodian in Panama and had driven out to pick up his parents in Johnson City. Now, on that crisp autumn day, James and Ruby were gathered together in the sight of God and both families (including Ruby's three brothers) to be wed in holy matrimony. The couple spent their honeymoon night at the house and then drove Flora and Thomas back to Johnson City.

When James and Ruby arrived at his parents' house, there awaited a wonderful surprise: a new Model A Ford. Flora had saved up her money, 150 dollars, which "about took all of her bank account." Flora and Thomas Jeremiah themselves did not acquire their own cars and driver's licenses until both of their sons had left the house. James commented later, "They probably waited to buy the cars until we were gone because they didn't want us to wreck them."

They spent the rest of that honeymoon day buzzing and rocking, jumping and rambling down interstate 17, a two-lane asphalt highway that stretched two hundred miles or more—all the way to Panama and to James' first call to full-time ministry.

In Panama, James meekly walked up to the door of a deacon's home, his once-combed-and-pushed-back hair now flaring out at different places. The drive had been long and loud, but full of anticipation of what God would do and gladness over what He had already accomplished. As he stretched his limbs, James tried to smooth out his rumpled shirt and pants, creased and wrinkled from the many miles of driving.

"Knock again," suggested Ruby, she, too, stepping out of the car to stretch and primp herself for her first meeting with the deacon. The wind blew cold from Canada, the dark and dried leaves crunching under both their feet. James lifted the tarnished knocker, but before he could tap it against the plate, the door swung wide open.

"Good afternoon, Elder," greeted Mr. Eddie, an old weathered-looking man, his face beaming with more anticipation than his newly arrived pastor.

James hesitated and turned to Ruby, then back to Mr. Eddie. *Elder?* thought James to himself, *Do I look that old to him?*

"Yes, yes, good to have you here," continued the old man, waving them both into the house.

Ruby covered her mouth to hide her astonished grin. James caught the smile and shrugged his shoulders as if to say, "I have no idea why he's calling me that."

Mr. and Mrs. Eddie were from the "old school" of Baptists, where the pastor was always referred to as "Elder." They had already cleaned out a room in their house for the young couple to stay while Harmony Baptist Church found them adequate living arrangements. James had arrived full circle: a rural community, where farming was the mainstay and long distances were the norm.

A Thrilling Thing

The world that James and Ruby Jeremiah entered in 1936 is far removed from today's readers, who take for granted nearly every comfort and convenience. In fact, it was a blessing for James to even get a job as fast as he did and with the stability and support that his had. "Six months after graduating from high school, over one in four males in New York State in 1936 was still unemployed, and one in seven was employed only part-time or seasonally."[12] On average it took two or more years to find a job.[13] James' weekly pay was $11.50, $46 a month, or $552 a year. This salary was far below the average of $1,160.[14] In an age when a yearly income of $1,000 would get a family by, James and Ruby had to depend completely upon the Lord and His provisions outside their meager allowance. And once again God showered His blessings upon them.

Panama, New York, was a poor farming community, a lifestyle that James was familiar with from his days as a boy growing up in Corning. The people of Harmony Baptist Church rallied around their new pastor with vigor. They could not pay him as much as they wanted, but they made up for it with special favors. Mrs. Eddie would gather eggs from her henhouse and walk them over every week to the Jeremiahs (now living in a small parsonage). Ruby was delighted with such a gesture and invited the old woman in for coffee or tea and to share in a week's worth of conversation.

Ministry, reaching people with the gospel of Jesus Christ, was a hard and time-consuming task in Panama. The church was small and dying and in desperate need of new, fresh souls who were ready to serve their Lord. James realized that a vibrant Sunday School was a necessity for potential growth and for the longevity of the church. His own life had been radically altered by his experience with such a place, and Harmony Baptist Church, if it were going to be effective, had to establish some sort of outreach to the rural children in the community. So there were business meetings and more business meetings. For such a small church, the congregation loved to have meetings. The deacons prayed for the means while James actively pursued (as he would do all of his life) his vision for development. One day, it all came together.

On the outskirts of town stood an abandoned building by an old sawmill. James was able to work with the deacons, and the church bought the property. Soon James had it fixed up and running as a Sunday School. A key to any successful institution (obviously the working of the Holy Spirit is essential) is publicity. Every day James would go out into the fields, into the farmyards, and into the houses and witness to his community, talking to the parents and the children about the church and the new Sunday School building. It was the children, not the parents, who began to show up little by little. In a town of about 300 souls, witnessing and growth were hard to come by.

One evening while James was sitting down to read, he heard a knock at the door. Ruby peered out the window. It was a member of the congregation. James and Ruby did not own a telephone and "didn't want the church to buy one; they could not afford it." James would laughingly relate years later, "It is amazing what you can escape when you don't have one of those things."

Ruby opened the door with a warm smile, but immediately squelched it, for the woman on the porch was frantic.

"You must get Pastor!" cried the woman hysterically. "It's Mr. Eddie! He is not well!"

Pastor Jeremiah hurried off to the Eddies' home. As he rushed up the driveway, he reflected on the time nearly a year and a half ago that he and Ruby had arrived for the first time at that quaint house, that autumn eve with the turning leaves. James rushed through the all-too-familiar living room, sweeping by several of the neighbors, and made his way to where the old man lay. And then he stopped cold. He covered his mouth, a terrible fear buckling his knees. James desperately composed his thoughts. He was a pastor, a leader, a shepherd to his flock. What he did next would either calm or create more fear. There, sprawled out across the dining room table, mouth open, body stiff from a seizure, lay poor Mr. Eddie. He had had a stroke, and by the look of the surroundings, had tried with some desperate effort to pull himself from the table. Mrs. Eddie sobbed near her departed husband's head, and her behavior compelled James to take up his role as comforter. Meanwhile, everyone waited for the doctor. What a heavy blow for such a young pastor. Mr. Eddie's funeral was to be James' first as a minister of the Lord, and his Home-going was the third of several losses that would reside in James' mind for the rest of his life.

Death is that constant chorus, a great and horrible reminder chiding the believer and unbeliever alike, over and over and over that we are strangers and wanderers in a world that was not made for our keeping. We are temporary lights to a dark place, lights that will someday, sooner or later, walk on a new earth and in a new Heaven. During his first years as a pastor at Harmony Baptist Church, James would face death in several guises, even "a couple of babies." How often must he have thought of his brother Howard during such times!

It was during his second year at Harmony Baptist Church in Panama that James began to feel restless. He started to mention to Ruby more and more consistently and with great vigor his need for further education, perhaps traveling all the way to Illinois and Wheaton College. They plodded along with the daily ups and downs of pastoring a small rural church, but left a door open to see where the Lord wished them. Panama was more successful (a place with some vision for missions, evangelism, church growth) than when James had arrived. The church membership and Sunday School classes were holding their own. James had even tried a "Bible class in a home to get some of the citizens of Panama to come." It worked. And the church family would soon grow by one more in another way.

The Christmas season of 1937 found Ruby pregnant. And as she carried the baby to term, the new parents were delighted and thrilled with the awe and wonder over what lay ahead. On September 7, 1938, James drove Ruby to Corry, Pennsylvania, across the state line, to the nearest hospital. Ruby delivered with no complications their first child, and they named the precious little girl Loisanne. And when Ruby was able to come home, James proudly brought mother and daughter back to the parsonage in Panama. The new addition was wondrous and at the same time invoked anxiety for the new couple. Loisanne meant another mouth to feed. Yet, as so many times before, God provided all the family's needs. James was ready for fatherhood, and he jumped into his new role with all that he had. But still the restlessness induced by the Holy Spirit clawed at him. It was March 1939 when the Lord indicated a move.

James had held evening services since he had begun his pastorate at Panama. They never did quite excel in attendance. So he decided that instead of the Sunday evening service, he would make better use of his time traveling to area churches, preaching, evangelizing, and building up the body of Christ. A church in Jamestown, New York, was in need of just such help, and James gladly accepted the challenge. Well, some of "the old boys who were not even going to evening service got pretty disturbed and decided to have a meeting to discuss it."

During that same time S. Franklin Logsdon, then pastor of Bethel Baptist Church in Erie, Pennsylvania (soon to become the pastor at Moody Church in Chicago), called James on the telephone and said, "I want to recommend

A Thrilling Thing

you to a church in Toledo." James and Franklin had become quite good friends during James' stay in Panama. It was at Franklin's church that James broadcast his first radio message. James had spoken with Franklin many times about his ambition for further education, so Franklin's phone call came as quite a surprise. There was a long silence on the phone. James responded, "I don't know if I'm interested," then his voice boomed with joy, "because I've been accepted at Wheaton College, and I want to go there to finish my education." Franklin's voice was excited as well, for he knew how much his friend desired this next step. There was another pause, and James replied, "Franklin, I will do whatever God wants me to do."

So Franklin Logsdon, moved by the Holy Spirit, recommended James T. Jeremiah to Emmanuel Baptist Church in Toledo. Nothing happened. Like all crossroads in our lives, God's ways are not our ways, and His timing is rarely our timing. While they remained in Panama, the door stayed open for James and Ruby to be able to leave New York and move to Wheaton, Illinois. In the meantime, a call came from Toledo, "Would you be interested in coming to preach at our church?" James grabbed the opportunity and traveled to Emmanuel Baptist in Ohio.

Toledo was like nothing James had experienced before: big, inner city, alive, thousands of people, a completely overwhelming environment to a pastor from rural New York. He preached his message in the old building, had a "delightful time," and drove home. He was scared out of his wits and wanted more than ever to go to Wheaton, which he pictured as safe in the cloistered confines of a college filled with believers, far from the maddening, needy urban crowds of the city. And now James and Ruby were uncertain: stay in Panama (the church was growing; it was manageable), go to Wheaton and receive a college education, or take up a pastorate in Toledo (which at the time had

45

not yet been offered). They just had to trust and obey, take the steps of obedience, and not be afraid.

Meanwhile, the evening service situation in Panama had come to a head. Several of the members (the ones who never went to the evening service and rarely made it to the morning one) had decided to call James on the carpet. They were to have yet another business meeting the coming Sunday afternoon to discuss what to do about their pastor. James got wind of what was happening, that some really divisive individuals were going to stir up trouble. And it just so happened that on the Saturday before the meeting, he received a call from Emmanuel Baptist in Toledo: they wanted him to be their pastor.

"So I decided that on that Sunday I would preach and then read them my resignation." James preached a fiery sermon, prayed, and then suddenly looked up at the congregation and said, "Sit down, folks. We are going to have a business meeting." The congregation erupted with murmurs and looks of astonishment. This was not the way things were to be done. The troublemakers in the group, too, sat dumbfounded. After reading his letter of resignation, James folded the paper, gathered his Bible and notes, and walked down the aisle separating the stunned congregation.

The treasurer of the church, who worked for the phone company and who had not been present at the service, walked in that morning to gather up the offering, and then immediately ran over to the parsonage.

"What in the world did you do there this morning?" she demanded, befuddled.

"Why do you ask?" responded James with a sly smile.

"Well," continued the treasurer, "I went in to collect the offering, and found everyone just sitting there, silent. They don't know what to do!"

James would remember that scene years later: "I think

those old boys thought that they had it all prepared to do. I don't know what would have happened, but I would have said, 'If you want me here, you get here. Fair enough?' "

Although James' action sounds dramatic—and at the time it was—no long-term damage occurred. In fact James and Ruby would return to that church in Panama many times, always to a warm and welcoming congregation.

God had just pushed a cautious young man and his family to the next step in a long, arduous, and fulfilling life. In Toledo James would face his second challenge and come face-to-face with the slippery precipices of a large inner city church, a church that would stretch him to the extent of his being. James did not want to go to Toledo, but God usurped his desires. And now, once again, he had to make the choice to be obedient. "You look back and you ask, 'Why, Lord?' The reasons at the time you don't know. But God has His reasons. It is a thrilling thing, brother, to look back and see the workings of God in your life."

ENDNOTES

1. All quotations of James T. Jeremiah, unless otherwise noted, are from personal interviews conducted by the author.
2. *The Seminarion, 1935* (Johnson City, N.Y.: Baptist Bible Seminary, 1935), 35, 40.
3. Ibid., 39.
4. Ibid.
5. Ibid.
6. Victor Bondi, ed. *American Decades: 1930–1939* (Detroit: Gale Research Inc., 1995), 13.
7. Ibid., 14.
8. *Seminarion*, 28.
9. Ibid.
10. Ibid., 28.
11. Ibid., 36.
12. *American Decades: 1930–1939,* 328.
13. Ibid.
14. Ibid., 315.

Chapter 3

A Sound from Heaven
(1939–1953)

On September 1, 1939, German forces slammed into Poland from Silesia, East Prussia, and Slovakia. There were 1.5 million men (52 divisions) against a Polish army a third that size. Germany unveiled the blitzkrieg—highly mobile tactical aircraft leading the ground force through and around the Polish defenses.[1] World War II was on. The world, including the United States, would never be the same again:

> The 1940's were a decade in which history dramatically transformed the lives of millions, radically altering basic suppositions about the character and possibility of life itself. The period following the war brought an explosion of monographs on religion, psychological studies of authoritarianism, and novels dissecting the war experience.... While intellectuals revised basic social and political assumptions, average people grappled with the disruption of established norms caused by the war.... Americans never experienced the terror of air bombardment, the loss of homes, the suspension of justice.... Instead, [they] emerged from the war as citizens of the most powerful nation on earth, far more prosperous than they were before it. People's ambitions, their expectations and desires, however, had been altered irrevocably. Americans spent the first five years of the decade watching the world pull their lives apart; they spent the

next five years of the decade trying to put their lives back together. But nothing was ever the same.[2]

In 1939, James, Ruby, and Loisanne Jeremiah arrived in Toledo, a waterfront city on the coast of Lake Erie. The expectations were high, the fear and anxiety higher. While James struggled to console and gather his new flock, Toledo's sons and daughters were making ready for war.

In a way, James had been prepared for this move more than any other, for this church had at one time been pastored by Dr. Earle G. Griffith, a former president of Baptist Bible Seminary. James' respect for Griffith and his willingness to "show himself approved" drove James forward in determining how to advance the gospel in such a world and in such desperate times. Since church attendance had fallen off precipitately, and since the present congregation had little money to give, James struck up an agreement with his deacons: "They gave us $25, plus half of everything that came in: $49 in the general fund."[3] At the beginning of his ministry in Toledo, this amount was hardly enough to live on, but after just one year the church began to grow to the point that James thought that his current scale "would not do"; he was making too much money. And he was right. In just a few months, behind his careful direction, the church had grown out of their building. He asked the deacons to establish a set salary for him, and they did. The Lord had placed His hand upon the church, and people were coming to place their faith in Christ. It was time for a new building. James would recall later that Emmanuel Baptist Church of Toledo "started in a shack building on the corner of Oakwood and Detroit Avenue." It was a small building for 175 people and boasted a small balcony; "it was an old church." The move would soon put the congregation to the test.

From his early years growing up in Corning, New York,

A Sound from Heaven

James Jeremiah had always been intrigued with the concept of wire communications. He recalled years later the long telephone lines draping like loops of string across the small town, lines that fell down with each windstorm. And of course there was the telephone:

> The telephone hung on the wall. It took the place of a radio. Whenever it rang, you would go over, pick it up and listen to anything anybody was saying. The people calling each other could hear what you said, but there was the possibility that they didn't; and you could listen to the news of the community. I didn't do this, but I knew it was being done.

But it was the radio—a wooden box, a mysterious alchemist that converted pulses of electricity into life—that really captured James' imagination. "I remember when our neighbor got a radio. This fellow was not wealthy, but he had an uncle who lived in Hawaii and gave it to them as a Christmas present." James' mother and father would go up to the neighbor's house on weekends to play cards, to chat, and every now and then to listen to the latest radio drama or music. And James also would stop over at that house each day after school. There, Aunt Mary (a name the kids gave to the kindly neighbor) would give him a drink of water. The radio would be hissing out stories, music, and news. The Jeremiah family "finally got a radio. Boy, was that something. You can't imagine what that was like."

But just listening to radio dramas and music was not enough for James. "Then I got the idea that I would build one. So I made a little radio when I was a kid. It worked. I got the parts and put it together. It seemed to do all right, and was not as loud as the others." Later he constructed a shortwave radio.

James Jeremiah was one of the first pastors to use this medium in the Toledo area. His goal was to reach as many people as he could, and with it perhaps his church would grow. "Radio was big. People listened. I felt that if I could get a message across, people would come to church and get saved." This "need for promotion" and "getting the message across" would be hallmarks of his long and distinguished career as pastor and eventually as president of Cedarville College.

"When I got to Toledo, I recognized the need to try to acquaint people with our church. So we started a radio program called *The Bible Breakfast Time*." This was a big investment for such a small struggling church, and they had to raise the money to buy all the equipment to broadcast. Until the money was raised, James "would travel downtown at 7:00 every morning to 5,000-watt station WSPD and host a fifteen-minute program." People did start receiving the message, did start coming through the doors, and the once struggling church desperately needed space to seat them. *The Bible Breakfast Time* audience was receptive to James' messages for several reasons. First, it was the "golden age" of radio. The 1940s was the last decade in which radio was the dominant medium of information and entertainment.[4] After World War II, television would come to dominate the airwaves. Second, the pastor's radio broadcasts dealt with themes that were becoming more important to people: depravity, salvation, family, moral fortitude, and good and evil. The world was at war, and with war comes a desperate search for answers:

> After a long period of decline during the Depression, American churches experienced a revival . . . following World War II. Church membership skyrocketed, and thousands of new congregations were formed. About 43 percent of the public attended church before the war; by 1950 more than 55 percent were members of religious groups, a figure that would increase to 69 percent by the end of the 1950s.[5]

A Sound from Heaven

Pastor Jeremiah and his deacons formed a committee to acquire a new building to meet their own membership growth. The building that they were in was "a small thing, but it had a good location because Detroit Avenue was a thoroughfare." To hurry things along, the committee decided that they would buy a vacant duplex next to the church. The church revamped that building but immediately filled it. Soon, as before, they were looking for ample space. Then the pastor caught wind of a perfect, available location just down the road: First Church of Christ, Scientist.

One could barely find two more divergent congregations in Toledo than Emmanuel Baptist Church and the Christian Science Society. The building had possibilities for expansion and was in a perfect location—just down the road. When Emmanuel Baptist decided to buy the building, James had to raise a substantial amount of capital for a down payment. So the church agreed they would sell their property first and then purchase the building from the Christian Scientists.

Just before the deacons were to close the deal on the building, several overly enthusiastic members of the congregation decided to visit the new space. It was located on a perfect lot on a major highway going out of the city. The members were impressed with the location, with the potential, and even with what they considered a testimony to buy it from a heretical group. But it seemed to some of them that just buying the building might not be evangelistic enough. So while they toured the place, they tried to remedy the situation. The group left, pleased with the opportunity to serve the Lord and more pleased with the building that was soon to be theirs.

"What do you mean you won't sell us the building!" roared James Jeremiah the following day. The leader of the Christian Scientists was on the phone.

"There are tracts in every one of our hymnals!" screamed back the leader. "We were having our service, and members of the congregation began pulling those blasted things out all over the place!" There was a pause, and then a huff. "The deal is off," the voice shouted. "We would not sell this building to you if you were the last people on earth!" James was about to speak and was cut off. "I have never been so insulted in all my life! Never! Even if you were the last . . . I mean the last people on earth!" The phone clicked, followed by a dial tone.

There would be no new building. Furthermore, reconciliation would be useless; the bridge to that location was still smoldering. Now what were they to do? Not only did Emmanuel Baptist have a building problem, James was faced with finding a place to meet the following Sunday. The previous church had been sold: they were a congregation without a place to worship. After a few phone calls, James was able to secure the old sanctuary for one last meeting.

As the congregation gathered, there was a sense of disbelief, a stunned silence. All this time they had prayed for a place, and God had seemingly answered their prayers. What had happened? James stood before his congregation, opened his Bible to Genesis 50:20 and 21 and read:

> And Joseph said unto them, "Fear not: for am I in the place of God? . . . Ye thought evil against me; but God meant it unto good, to bring to pass, as it is this day, to save much people alive. Now therefore fear ye not. . . ."

Everyone needed to hear this message. A sense of peace settled upon the congregation. God's glory would be shown; He was moving, and nothing was too big for Him. That week James received another lead. This time it was for an old mansion, which was located directly across from the Christian Science building and had several acres of prop-

A Sound from Heaven

erty with it. "It was a big stone building with not a whole lot of room for addition." Everyone concerned wondered, *Will we be able to convert this huge house into a usable space for worship, fellowship, and Sunday School classes?* Emmanuel Baptist soon had at their disposal "an auditorium, a balcony that could seat 200 people, a big front room, a parlor that was a big-sized thing, and a lot of facilities that we could use for Sunday School." The mansion even had a "place in the back that was an apartment over a garage." This would become the Jeremiahs' new parsonage. The facility was more than they ever could have hoped for: a large yard, spacious rooms, and plenty of places for Loisanne (and the rest of the children soon to come).

A beautiful picture of James and his mother and mother-in-law shows the splendor of the small garden behind the house. Sitting in front of James is an aging and worn Flora, holding Loisanne on her lap, while James and his mother-in-law stand behind her. In the background flourish shrubs and wild flowers of many varieties, and several trellises don the entryway to the back door. In another picture, probably taken on that same visit, Flora (still holding Loisanne) stands next to a young, wavy-haired James on one side and Ruby, wearing a white coat and flowered dress, on the other side. This picture also displays a rich scene of large trees, lush flowers, neatly trimmed yard—a quiet and quaint city neighborhood in downtown Toledo.

The newly renovated building had its advantages, including the study. James would comment years later, "The study, brother! Not many Baptist preachers had this—it was covered with hardwood paneling, and oh, how quiet."

The congregation really worked together; they had a "willingness to work, trying to get people saved. All that sort of thing." James commented years later, "I think of all that the church people gave when making those moves.

Think about it—a gang of people with no building, and there were no complaints when we found a place that was no better than the place we had come from." And this was during the stresses of war. James recalls,

> It was a sad time because every day you would pick up the paper: what's going to happen next? What's going to happen to our country? What are we going to do? Fortunately, there were enough encouraging signs that we could go on to the next day. Hitler was a threat. I am sure that our government knew a lot more than the papers let on, but they would not tell us that. So you had to live in wonder . . . a daily agony.

President Roosevelt signed the Emergency Price Control Act on January 30, 1942, resulting in the rationing of all goods and commodities sold on the retail market.[6] "You couldn't run the car everywhere. You had to get tickets or points. You couldn't overdo it, you see. Visitation needs were a problem, and there were food problems sometimes." Sugar and coffee were the first items to use coupons; then "in early 1943 the OPA began a point-ration plan that applied to meat, fats and oils, cheese, and processed foods. Shoes were later rationed under the point system as well."[7]

Ruby would grow as many vegetables as she could in her Victory garden behind the house and then wait in line at the store with all the other wives, using her stamps to buy necessary essentials for her family:

> The OPA issued books of ration stamps with numbers of points printed on them and then assigned specific point values to rationed items. To replenish their stock, grocers sent the stamps to the local bank and got credit to buy more food. The average grocer had to handle some 3.5 billion tiny stamps each month. Sometimes they ran out of the gummed sheets on which they were supposed to stick the stamps. One wholesaler had to haul loose stamps to the bank in bushel baskets.[8]

A Sound from Heaven

"We never bypassed the rules," reminisced James. "We had enough to eat, the kids were able to live quite well. . . . As I look back on it, and all that those people went through, we suffered very little." Indeed, in spite of rationing,

> Americans ate better during the war than before. In 1943, despite the rationing of meat, meat consumption rose to 128.9 pounds per person per year. The Department of Agriculture reported that in 1945, Americans ate more food than at any other time in history. By the end of 1945 rationing of everything except sugar had ended.[9]

James' radio program soared in its listenership during the war. "I think our nation did a great job. I am an American. . . . Hitler was a satanic man. It was a horrible thing, and you knew it was then—the thing he was doing to the Jews." People were asking the tough questions, and *The Bible Breakfast Time* was answering them.

James did not serve overseas in the war. "I had a child, and I was a pastor and felt that I had a responsibility to the church and my family. I would have gone if I had been drafted, but they wouldn't draft me." Several people close to the Jeremiah family had entered the war effort, however. Edward Jeremiah, five years younger, signed up and ended up fighting in the Philippines, repairing aircraft blades and seeing firsthand the carnage on the beaches and the destructive power of the Japanese army. James would write his brother weekly to encourage him with words from the Bible. But the war dug deep into Edward's heart and mind, so deep that it scarred him and his worldview for the rest of his life. The war also hit home in Emmanuel Baptist. "We had several of the congregation in the war." Fifty years later James would recall, "We tried to contact them. Several of them were killed. I can't remember their names, but it was a heart-wrenching thing for the people in the church." On another occasion, "There was a girl in the church who had a sweetheart in the war. The fellow drowned in the Pacific Ocean. I was glad that I could help her. It was a time when people needed help."

The radio program continued to grow. James was taping his broadcasts and "transferring the message onto a sixteen-inch disc." One day James received a call from a man out of state who had heard the radio broadcasts and wanted the pastor to come and candidate for an open position. James refused the invitation. The man then wrote to WSPD asking for several messages. The radio station sent him the large reels of tape. James found out later that he had candidated unknowingly for the position via reel-to-reel tape.

Ruby Jeremiah also had her hands full during the war years because on February 13, 1941, David was born. James has a wonderful picture capturing father and son on their way to church. They are posing on the front porch step. James is wearing his characteristic round wire-rimmed glasses, his hair still curly but thinning ever so slightly. And next to him stands young David, large round face, hair combed in a haphazard fashion, winter coat unbuttoned, standing two stairs above his father and still coming only to his shoulder. It is a photograph that seems to capture a happy mood: a proud son with his even prouder father beside him.

Two years after David's birth, on March 4, 1943, Maryalyce was born. The fourth and final child, Jim, would follow shortly after.

On December 16, 1944, the war took a serious turn against the Allies, and a wave of anxiety swept across the United States. "German general Karl Von Rundstedt launched an unsuccessful German offensive in the Ardennes. This 'Battle of the Bulge' was the last major German military offensive of World War II." By the end of December the Germans were pushed back, and the Allies began to sweep across Europe. On May 8, 1945, V-E Day was proclaimed when the German authorities finally surrendered, and World War II was over in Europe. With great joy, James Jeremiah announced the news to his assembly that Sunday. Clapping, shouting, and tears filled the auditorium. Then on August 6, 1945, the *Enola Gay* dropped the first atomic bomb on Hiroshima, Japan, "killing more than 50,000 people and leveling four square miles of the city." Two days later Nagasaki lay in ruin: 40,000 people killed. Japan unconditionally surrendered on August 15, 1945. World War II was over in the Pacific as well.

The aftermath of war brought a certain fear worldwide. The bombs of mass destruction had been released, and such a power could spell the potential end of man. If humans were depraved, then how could anyone stop such destructive force from falling into the wrong hands? On March 5, 1946, the "wrong hands" were defined by Winston Churchill in his famous speech at Westminster College in Fulton, Missouri: "An iron curtain [of Communism] had descended across the continent." As one war ended, another war, a "cold war," began to emerge. But for most Americans, the latter half of the 1940s was a time of rehabilitation, reunion, and spiritual healing.

One afternoon James received a phone call from a deacon in Dayton, Ohio. His church wanted James to candidate. "May I call you, Pastor," said the voice on the phone. "You'd better not," replied James, "because I am not going." He did not hear anything else about it for quite some time. Meanwhile, his children were growing up, the congregation was increasing, people were coming to saving faith in Jesus. *This is no place to leave!* he would think to himself, sitting quietly in his study. He was comfortable, productive, doing the work of the Lord.

But Dayton called again, and this time one of the deacons offered to take James around the harvest fields of the city. Again, the pastor was being reminded of lessons such as how God does not place us in situations that we cannot handle, but teaches us incrementally to trust in Him, to obey, to take the next step. James Jeremiah was no longer the youthful, green pastor witnessing out in the fields of New York. He was married, the father of four children, a growing presence in the community and in the General Association of Regular Baptist Churches. His radio ministry was becoming more and more successful. Would he be led of the Lord to go anywhere else?

One Sunday while he was preaching, James became distracted by the large group of teens in the balcony. They had begun a habit of sitting together each Sunday service, whispering, poking, laughing, fidgeting around. James had a real heart for them, for he had been converted fairly early in life and knew that the kids needed to pay attention, to be serious about the things of the Lord and about worshiping in the house of the Lord. So after the service, James hurried up to the balcony. He sat the teens down and said, "You young people have to change this now. Next week I want you either to sit with your parents . . . or to come and sit by me." He walked down the stairs from the balcony very impressed with his ultimatum. The following Sunday it soon became obvious who had won the battle of wills. James seated himself in the front pew. Just before the service began, he heard a loud shuffling of feet. The adolescents had decided to accept their pastor's invitation and sit with *him!*

One evening at the end of the decade while Ruby, James, and the children were gathered around the dinner table for family devotions, James opened the Bible to Acts 2:1 and 2:

> Now when the day of Pentecost was fully come, they were all with one accord in one place. And suddenly there came *a sound from heaven* as of a rushing mighty wind, and it

> filled all the house where they were sitting [emphasis added].

Suddenly, at that moment, the doorbell rang. David, without hesitation and with a touch of sarcasm, proclaimed, "Dad, that's the sound from Heaven!" James glanced sideways at his son, then strolled to the door. There, standing on the front porch was the postman with a special delivery letter with news: Emmanuel Baptist Church of Dayton had voted unanimously to call James Jeremiah as their new pastor. This was another defining moment in his life. God had asked again for James to take another step. "Dayton was a challenge to me. It would reach a lot of people. I didn't realize at the time that they had a radio program, but they had a good one. I don't know; I just felt that it was right in my heart." He discussed the move with his family. Ruby and James had been diligently praying for an answer for quite some time. "I had a wife who wanted me to be obedient. We had a family that was obedient. I mean, those kids were excited about what was to be done. . . . The whole family worked together. You can't explain it any other way than the hand of God."

James told his congregation the news the next Sunday and was met with a sigh of both understanding and remorse. The church was booming, and people were coming to the Lord. The congregation may have sensed that it would not be long until some other group would beckon such a leader.

For a number of years Emmanuel Baptist Church of Dayton had been known as the Haynes Street Baptist Church on Haynes and Parrott Streets. The building it occupied when James arrived had been purchased two years earlier from Memorial Presbyterian Church.[10] It was an enormous stone structure with a high-pitched roof and a three-story stone bell tower located on the corner of East Third Street. Perched nearly two stories high, just above the entrance, hung an enormous cross with "Emmanuel Baptist" scrolled down the stem and "Jesus Saves" across the top.

With a bit of fear and trembling but emboldened by the Holy Spirit, James took to the pulpit the first Sunday of January 1950. His message appropriately was "The Importance of a Great Beginning."[11] Behind him sat the choir, attentive; next to him sat Harold Engle, the music director. The preaching style that he had acquired over the years, a bold forthright approach, energized the congregation. There was a sense of "enthusiasm and personal responsibility not common among the larger churches" in the area.[12] The congregation was pleased, and James got on with the new decade doing what he had done so many times before: spreading the Word of God from his pulpit and behind the microphone of his radio program.

Emmanuel Baptist Church began to grow. "There [was] seemingly perfect peace among the people and a definite desire to reach souls for Christ."[13] James walked right into a radio program called *Back to the Bible Broadcast*, which had been airing for eight and a half years but which desperately needed revitalization. And that is what the new pastor brought to it. Again touching on the relevant, universal topics of redemption, personal sin, and the power and authority of Scripture, James began to build a ministry that first year, an unprecedented ministry in Dayton.

It was the radio program, most of all, that began to advertise and promote the church. James conducted his broadcast from WONE at 11:00 A.M. each day, Monday through Friday, and at 8:45 each Sunday morning. This ministry publicized the church throughout the city and was responsible for bringing many to the auditorium. The broadcast was reported from cities throughout Ohio. Several letters also were received from points in Kentucky and Indiana.[14]

Growth seemed to bring with it change. The church had

a "spacious parsonage adjacent to the church, which was located at 1500 Third Street; however, due to the rapid growth of the work and the pressing need for additional classroom space, as well as for development of the young people's work, the congregation decided to annex the building to the house of worship and purchase other property." And since the church was "located in a busy business district and the parsonage somewhat removed, [this was] to the definite advantage of the pastor and his family."[15]

James, Ruby, and the family (Loisanne, 12; David Paul, 10; Maryalyce, 7; and James Daniel, 3) moved into their new home, which was in an "exclusive residence district." The home contained seven large rooms, hardwood floors in good condition, automatic heat, air-conditioning equipment in the attic, and a sizable lot.[16]

As James' radio program increased along with the congregation, his presence within the Ohio Association of Regular Baptist Churches grew as well. In 1952, he found himself chairman of that organization and chairman of the council of the Fellowship of Baptists for Home Missions.[17] Above all of that, he had become a board member of Baptist Bible Institute in Cleveland.

The radio program had changed considerably since the early days in Toledo. *Back to the Bible Broadcast* was now aired directly from a desk in Emmanuel Baptist Church. The desk, located in the sanctuary, stood off to the side of the pulpit; and during the service, the whole apparatus sat under a sheet. The small wooden desk held turntables on either end. In the middle of the desktop stood a microphone, thin stem bent forward, bulbous head shaped like a huge bullet. In front of James on the paneled wall of the auditorium hung a round clock, and off to the left (at the very corner of the table) rested a radio. "The signal would come in on the radio, and then I would start talking. I would turn the radio down after I heard the announcement:

'Located out of Emmanuel Baptist Church, and now James Jeremiah will speak to you.' "

One day, James received a call from a woman in Arcanum, Ohio. It appears that she was so disgusted with the churches in the area and so pleased with the radio broadcasts from Emmanuel Baptist Church that she inquired if James would hold a Bible conference there. This conference would energize the people who were desperately trying to rid themselves of the liberal movement that had swept through the local churches. James agreed, and "about a year after that, I started going out every Thursday to Arcanum to hold a Bible study there." That ultimately became the seeds for Arcanum Baptist Church, located just ten miles or so from the Indiana border.

And there were still others who were touched by James' radio ministry. One such person was a prisoner in London, Ohio:

> These past few months have been quite an ordeal for me, but I know that it has been hard and trying for my wife. . . . I have enjoyed the good Christian fellowship and hearing of the true Word of God preached at Emmanuel Baptist Church, and I want to say right here and now that it has been of great help to me. I have been receiving the Sunday evening broadcast, and it has been a real blessing to my heart in hearing these services each Sunday night.[18]

The radio program not only helped those around the state, but it also served as a pragmatic impetus behind a successful Vacation Bible School. James has a picture, quite remarkable, in which all the church pews are filled with children of various ages—more than 280 young boys and girls of four and five, to older boys and girls of twelve and thirteen—some with their Sunday best on, others in T-shirts and jeans. The effect that Emmanuel Baptist Church began to have on the youth of Dayton, especially in the inner city, was unparalleled. There in the back of the photo, wearing small wire-rimmed glasses, arm around the back of a pew, sits James. "We had an unbelievable crowd coming. People were getting saved. It was something. I didn't want to leave."

James began speaking to churches on a regular basis, along with attending all the GARBC meetings. On one such occasion in 1951, James traveled to Oakland, California. He had become one of the representatives on the Council of Fourteen, along with distinguished members such as Joseph Stowell. At this particular conference, many addresses were given, but none more fervent than the one by Dr. Robert T. Ketcham over the extent of liberalism in the church. New associational literature would include "expositions on the historic principles and doctrines held by Baptists."[19] It would also emphasize separation from modernism. And this was the largest concern for GARBC churches in the 1950s. This tenacious upholding of doctrinal issues defined all of James' pastorates and his soon presidency at Cedarville College. "I am more concerned about maintaining the doctrine than the name. The doctrines are the things that count."

Doctrine had been an issue ever since his Baptist Bible Seminary days. In fact,

> When I was saved, our church in Johnson City was in the Northern Baptist Convention. There was going to be a meeting with the local churches. Dr. Harold Collins wanted us boys to go (some of us boys out of his classes). So we went. And the convention had an election of officers. The liberals presented a big list, and the fundamentalists presented a list. We had a judge there, Judge Remmington from Syracuse, New York. And he decided that we could not vote because we had not contributed to the convention. So, as I remember it, about 300 of us walked out of the prayer meeting.

> That was the end of the relationship between Binghamton, New York, and the Johnson City area.

As 1952 wound down, an interesting episode began to unfold all the way across the state, centered around Baptist Bible Institute in Cleveland. "The Hough Avenue Baptist Church, which housed the college, was an imposing structure . . . [but] had become inadequate for the expanding day school program," and the crime rate was escalating in the downtown area.[20] James was on the board of trustees for BBI, and the need for a new location had been on the table for quite some time. Several months passed, and then James decided to make a move.

Earlier, Harold Engles, Emmanuel's music director, had asked, "Preacher, do you think our school needs any property? Well, I'll tell ya. My dad lives in Cedarville. He told me that the school there is in a state that is unbelievable."

James recounts the rest:

> We went to see it, arranged to see the president. I whispered to Harold, "No Regular Baptist is going to move to this outfit." Harold suggested, "Why don't we wait to see what they do?" Thank God for good deacons. So we waited.

James and Harold had gone to see Cedarville College, a Presbyterian school that was in financial ruin and needed to be sold. James notified his fellow board members in Cleveland about the land and the school, but there seemed to be little interest. How could a Cleveland-based school just pack up and travel clear across the state to an unfamiliar site? "It took some convincing on [James'] part to get someone to come to Cedarville. Finally, 'it was decided that there would be no harm in appointing a committee to look over the property.' "[21]

Early in 1953 the board of BBI decided to "receive all Cedarville College property and take over the school's indebtedness."[22] Soon an agreement was struck between the two boards of trustees whereby "[Cedarville College would] [resign] and BBI [would] just take over."[23] The Dayton papers gave James the credit for the land transfer and being the major player behind the scenes who negotiated between the two schools. There was no money transfer, and the "Cleveland group [took] control of all [the college's] indebtedness and assets. The campus include[d] a 15-acre tract of land at the northern edge of town, and nine buildings. Most of the $160,000 endowment fund had been eaten up by operating deficits."[24]

Since James had been an integral part of the merger, he was soon named vice president of the college; and Dr. Leonard Webster, former president at BBI in Cleveland, was named president. The college had huge barriers to overcome if it were even to leave the ground, let alone fly. And as the first year progressed, it became apparent that the engines were sputtering, even before the plane left the runway.

Dr. Webster wrote an article for the *Ohio Independent Baptist* calling for money. "In December Webster informed the trustees that the college had outstanding bills of $24,074.83 with only 'slightly over $2,500 cash on hand.' "[25] And this debt was apparently the least of his worries. Several faculty members had written letters to the board expressing their dissatisfaction with the way Webster was running the school. The tidewaters burst the dam after the board from Cleveland went down to investigate:

> On Tuesday, December 15, the committee arrived in Cedarville. They spent three days investigating the situation in detail, and discovered Webster was living in a college residence which he had remodeled and repaired at college expense . . . paying neither rent nor utilities. . . . Further, they discovered the president's relationship to the faculty and

student body had deteriorated to the point that he had virtually no support in the college community.[26]

James had looked upon this whole situation with disdain and concern. He loathed seeing such an opportunity squandered, but the way the year had progressed, Cedarville College did not look promising. His own ministry at Emmanuel Baptist was thriving but nearly self-sufficient, for it had no choice: James was given increasingly more and more responsibilities as the ordeal with Webster began to unfold. Soon it was apparent that Dr. Leonard Webster must step down, and that turn of events would mean that the responsibility of the college lay with the vice president. The college had become a hornet's nest of unrest. Conflicts were breaking out among faculty, students, and even the Cedarville local community. In human terms, to take on a task of leading such a place would be ludicrous, especially for a man whose church and ministry were thriving. What did James Jeremiah know about the world of academics? No, this was for someone else. James tried to keep the fires to a minimum and prayed to God for guidance. God's answer was soon apparent, and James was not too happy about it.

"Call unto me, and I will answer thee, and shew thee great and mighty things, which thou knowest not" (Jeremiah 33:3).

ENDNOTES

1. These facts were taken from a fantastic chronology of World War II: *World War II Almanac, 1931–1945* (New York: G. P. Putnam's Sons), 90.

2. Victor Bondi, ed. *American Decades: 1940–1949* (Detroit: Gale Research Inc., 1995), vii.

3. All quotations of James T. Jeremiah, unless otherwise noted, are taken from interviews conducted by the author.

4. Bondi, 362.

5. Ibid., 449.

6. Ibid., 338.
7. Ibid., 339.
8. Ibid.
9. Ibid.
10. "Dayton Baptist Church Picks New Pastor," *Dayton Journal Herald*, 28 December 1949.
11. *Dayton Daily News*, 31 December 1949.
12. "Parsonage Dedication," *The Ohio Independent Baptist*, December 1950.
13. Ibid.
14. Ibid.
15. Ibid.
16. Ibid.
17. *Dayton Journal Herald*.
18. Inmate in London, Ohio, to James Jeremiah, 22 July 1953.
19. "Sunday School Literature Plan Related at Baptist Conclave," *Oakland Tribune*, 16 May 1951.
20. J. Murray Murdoch, *Cedarville College: A Century of Commitment*, (Cedarville, Ohio: Cedarville College, 1987), 95. This is an excellent text on the history of Cedarville College. J. Murray Murdoch writes with candor and style in this definitive work.
21. Ibid., 85.
22. *Dayton Daily News*, 16 March 1953.
23. Ibid.
24. *Dayton Daily News*, 5 April 1953.
25. Murdoch, 98.
26. Ibid., 100.

Chapter 4

The Reluctant President
(1953–1961)

In 1953, the newly revived Cedarville College found itself in utter chaos. The base of its constituency never had time to develop, leadership was nonexistent, and the relationship with the community had all but decayed. James T. Jeremiah was apprised of this situation, for he was the only locally situated member on the board of trustees. He had been made vice president of the college for that very reason, and was expected to keep his finger on the pulse of the institution and keep the board informed. But his pastorate was his forté: "I had a great church, a great life, a Vacation Bible School with more than 600 kids. We were building a new building, and I had a very successful radio program. I was having a ball."[1] His position of vice president was little more than a figurehead.

"Webster had taught up at the Cleveland school (Baptist Bible Institute). He got to Cedarville in June; by November he was out." Dr. Leonard Webster had cut asunder any bonds that had grown between him and the faculty. By the time James was able to assess the situation on campus, the faculty were ready to resign. The college needed a leader, someone who could pull and push the struggling college into uncharted waters.

James recounts an unfortunate incident: One of the professors (a Ph.D.) counseled a female student. "Well, she came out of his office crying. He had classified her as a lesbian. This almost gave her mother a heart attack! We were going to have a board meeting to deal with him. Webster was the sitting president. The professor in question had an appointment to meet before the committee. He didn't show. Webster told me to go find him. So I went over to the old gym, found him, and asked him why he hadn't shown. He said, 'Well, I came on your time, and you weren't ready; so you can wait for my time.' And I responded, 'You get over there now! Not any other time but now!' I never in my life had spoken to anyone like that."

There were moments like this one, when James found himself being more than a behind-the-scenes vice president and having to act like an authoritarian. "I felt sorry for Webster, but I certainly did not want his job." As the extent of corruption and discord surfaced, the board soon realized that Webster was doing "crazy outlandish things . . . ; the faculty was disgusted and wished him gone." James began to take on more and more responsibilities on campus and did most of the presidential work during the months the board was negotiating with Webster.[2] Soon it was apparent that if the college were to survive, James T. Jeremiah would have to assume the role of acting president while the board looked for a replacement.

James was not in the least bit interested in the position of president. God had called him to be a pastor, to preach the Word of God. He felt compelled to spread the gospel in every new location he had accepted, and God had certainly blessed him and his congregations. As his "interim presidency" wobbled forward, James, "sort of tried to help" as best he was able, and his "good relationship with the faculty" helped considerably. "One of the professors, Arthur Williams, had taught me at Baptist Bible Seminary, and we were always good friends."

Meanwhile, the board of trustees searched for qualified candidates to fill the open position at the college. "No less

1. Wedding portrait of Flora Augusta (Rozell) and Thomas Jeremiah

2. Flora and James, 1915

3. James at age 3, 1917

4. Howard Jeremiah, 1924

5. Howard Jeremiah one year before he died, 1925

6. Mary Jane Rozell and Edward Stanley Rozell. James and his family moved in with them in Johnson City after Howard's death.

7. Ruby, Loisanne, Flora, and James in Panama, New York

8. James fresh out of Baptist Bible Seminary

9. James Jeremiah, a young pastor in Toledo

10. James and older son, David, 1946

11. Flora and Thomas Jeremiah with grandson Jim in Toledo

12. The Jeremiah family in the 1940s

13. Jeremiah family portrait

14. Ruby Jeremiah celebrating her birthday in Toledo

15. James and friends celebrating Ruby's birthday

16. Ruby and James in Toledo

17. James posing in the basement of Founders Hall, where he and others made the bricks for construction projects on the Cedarville College campus

18. James and Ruby posing in 1973 next to the motor home given to them by the Cedarville College board of trustees

19. James and Ruby helping to transfer library books from the old Cedarville College library to the new one

20. Dedication plaque presented to James after Ruby's death.

21. James and his brother Edward

22. James and Ethel Jeremiah

23. James T. Jeremiah

The Reluctant President

than seven other individuals were contacted for the position of 'acting president,' " with James becoming the liaison between many of them and the board.³

And as all of this desperation was occurring on the campus of Cedarville College, the people of Emmanuel Baptist Church of Dayton were excitedly stepping forward toward the completion of their new building, "costing in excess of $112,000."⁴ During the dedication of the enormous addition to the existing church, James wrote in the church bulletin:

> Many church building programs have been a heartache to the pastor and those who work with him. I am personally grateful to the board of our church for the way they have carried the burden of this venture of faith. We have had, and still have great problems to face, but each one of the officers of the church [has] undertaken great responsibilities without desire for personal gain or glory.⁵

The resonance between the two institutions cannot be lost on the reader. While one was struggling for its very existence, the other was giving thanks to God for supplying all its needs. James' references to the problems that the people of Emmanuel Baptist were facing foreshadowed not only that he would leave but also, in a personal way, what he would soon face.

In June 1954, James' name was presented to the board of trustees as a candidate for "acting president," and James expressed four conditions, as recorded by J. Murray Murdoch, a professor at Cedarville College:

> First, he would insist that the training offered would be evangelistic in emphasis and that we would train your people in the matter of church building. Second, he would *not* take a job that would keep him from preaching. Third, the trustees would be responsible to help him get openings in churches. [And]

> fourth, he would require that the college launch out into a definite direct mail program using various types of literature to promote the school, and have some sort of printing or offset printer of our own to prepare this literature.⁶

In September 1954, Pastor Jeremiah refused the offer of such a position, stating mainly this:

> The title "acting president" suggests the idea of a temporary arrangement. The Cedarville community and our churches across the country are bound to get this impression. *Mail continues to come to the school addressed to two former "acting presidents" of the college. For a number of years the townspeople have been aware of the temporary leadership given to the college. This unfavorable reaction of the people in Cedarville was recently expressed to me by one of the leading citizens* [emphasis added].⁷

This wise perception separated James Jeremiah from the other candidates and former presidents of the college. The "unfavorable reaction of the people in Cedarville" was a most candid observation of one reason for the school's severe problems. The division between the primarily Presbyterian community and the new Baptist intruders ran deep. From headlines such as "Baptists Save College" to the ineptness in governing of the first president who took office from the former Presbyterian College president, all eyes of the community had been watching the unwanted guests. James knew that if he were to be appointed "acting president," a message would again come across clear and strong: the place is not going to make it. Further, nobody wants to be a part of a losing team, nor do they wish to contribute money or children to a place that may fold. Very few desire to help save a dying institution, but many will gladly jump aboard the wagon once it is stable and rolling along. James'

The Reluctant President

decline of the invitation forced the board (including himself) to search for someone who was willing to give his every ounce toward the school's success.

James had been getting candid advice from those whom he trusted as his name was being circulated as president for the college. Mead Armstrong, a good friend from Johnson City, told him,

> It will never go. It will never work. They've lost their recognition. They've never had accreditation, and they have lost their teacher training. Jim, it will never go; it will die. . . .

Dr. Paul Jackson, president of Baptist Bible Seminary, warned, "Don't take it. Don't be president of that thing. Don't do it, Jim. It will kill you."[8]

Then the inevitable happened: the board of trustees reworded the offer previously extended to Pastor Jeremiah and asked him to be president of Cedarville College. With such negative opinions offered by their friends, James and Ruby had real concerns. Ruby exclaimed years later, "Jim tried everybody he knew to try to get them to come, but nobody would come. I didn't blame them. Really, we didn't want to either."[9]

"Everything I have had in the ministry—every church, every school, every faculty—started as low as it can go. One nice thing about that is it's easy to start and see results. God has been good to me." The mountain before James was immense, staggeringly so.

The small church in Panama, his first pastorate, had been a challenge—more of a stepping-stone. The call to Toledo had been a higher mountain, yet there the radio ministry really began. The call to Dayton had been a phenomenal success: a new building, a dynamic radio ministry, amazing church growth, and hundreds of people coming to know the saving grace of Jesus.

But now came a completely different calling. This was

academics, a completely new animal. This was liberal arts education. James would not be presiding over parishioners from every walk of life but highly trained and disciplined minds that knew a lot more about their fields than he did. Cedarville College was a financially ruined, community-deserted institution. But God was calling James and his family to obedience. And as Ruby so deftly proclaimed, "We didn't dare do anything else."[10] So James accepted the challenge to become president of Cedarville College. The *Dayton Daily News* notified the people of Dayton about the changing of the guard at the small college, and the *Ohio Independent Baptist* shouted it statewide:

> The days of uncertainty are over, and the administration at the college moves forward boldly. Nine full-time members of the faculty are in service, one hundred and eleven students are in the classes, the finances are in much better condition, and there is an attitude of expectancy among the Regular Baptist people.[11]

The "days of uncertainty" were not over but just beginning, and in this article the enthusiasm behind the text can only be construed as one of the first moves by James to promote the "new" school and its sorely needed new image. He had learned through his pastorates, through his radio ministry, and through hard knocks that if he were to raise substantial amounts of money for the school, "you don't send out letters of despair if you want a response. The answer to that kind of thing is, 'If they are that bad off, why should I give to something that's going to die?' "[12]

On October 22, 1954, Emmanuel Baptist Church held a farewell service in honor of the Jeremiah family, and James and Ruby moved to Chillicothe Avenue in Cedarville with the school year already in session.

This new mountain, this new Herculean task before him, was nothing more than God appointed. James would laughingly remark later, "One of the things that thrills me more than anything about my life is the way God has taken care of me. If my high school teachers had still been living when I became president, they would have died soon thereafter."

But the deep divisions in the community and lingering divisions within the college itself continued. The Presbyterians primarily were anxiously watching the progress or failure of the newly acquired college.

"You see," explains James, "they had failed."

> And when we took the college over, I think they had the idea that we Baptists were going to not only take over the school but also fade into what they were doing in their churches, that is, become Presbyterians. But we didn't do that—we built our own church. And once that furor died down a bit, we bought one of their churches. The Presbyterians had failed, and that caused a lot of tension.

A perfect example of this animosity occurred when the local Presbyterian church was put up for sale. James, the new president, and the Baptists offered to buy it for $28,000. A Nazarene church offered $14,000, and in a backdoor move, the Presbyterians offered first bids to the latter, when for all intents and purposes the college had the higher offer. This action indicates how determined the Presbyterians were against allowing the Baptists to create a foothold in the town. The governing Presbyterian synod caught wind of the subversion and demanded that the Cedarville Presbyterian Church sell to the Baptists, the higher bidders.

"The people of the village of Cedarville knew little of the theological currents in the Baptist denomination. At the time of the transition, there was not even a Baptist church in the village."[13] The misconceptions and ill-formed rumors were all it took for the residents to distrust and criticize the new college and its mission. James would recall later how

"Ruby would go to the school, and the others in the parent-teacher organization would not talk to her. She was completely isolated." It would be a hard lesson to learn for both sides, but eventually after time and distance James would say, "I think we ought to take Bible-believing people over unbelievers. Denomination should not have anything to do with it." But the heart of James had always been Baptist to the core. He once commented that one day he was asked what he would have been had he not been raised Baptist. His response was concise and to the point: ashamed.

There were really four major problems or obstacles that James inherited as president of Cedarville College. The first has already been mentioned: the ties with the community; and, though not as significant as it may appear, this problem would be crucial later in the college's development. The second was the financial instability of the college, an overwhelming debt created by Webster and his lack of management. Third, and most critical, was Cedarville College's lack of credibility in the academic community. It was not accredited by the state of Ohio, and for it to gain any respect whatsoever, it had to obtain state certification. This would be an ongoing struggle, for the college had very few faculty members with doctorate degrees and some without master's degrees. Last, James Jeremiah and Cedarville College faced an onslaught of criticism within their own camp. Bob Jones University continually lambasted the college for trying to be a liberal arts college, a college (according to Bob Jones) that was walking along a slippery slope toward liberalism.

One of the major concerns that soon faced James was his personal lack of academic experience. How could he possibly promote the institution as one of excellence in the liberal arts and Bible when he himself did not have even a bachelor's degree? Baptist Bible Seminary neither was accredited by the State of New York, nor did it grant diplomas. When James graduated from that institution, he was handed a certificate in Bible. This was all he needed if spreading the Word of God were his mandate. But becoming president of the college suddenly placed him in the spotlight of the world of academics. In such a world the gospel is minimized, and one's credentials become the sole foundation for reputation. It mattered little that in the last seventeen years or so James had witnessed to thousands of people, organized and raised funds for large building projects, created from nearly nothing a very successful radio broadcast—no, none of this now mattered in the eyes of academicians across the state and to those very important people who could grant accreditation to the college. James knew that if he were to get the much-needed boost of accreditation, he would at least pursue and finish a bachelor's degree from somewhere.

At the moment, however, the school faced a serious drawback. The Education Department, a mainstay of the institution at the time, was producing teachers who could not find jobs in the state of Ohio, for the degree that Cedarville College offered was not sanctioned or even recognized by the state. Something had to be done, so James decided to visit the head of the Ohio Department of Education.

James drove to Columbus, sat in the office of the department head, and was promptly told that Cedarville College would need an endowment of at least $150,000. "Well, that was like saying $4 million to us." There was silence for a moment as the weight of that amount settled upon James. The head of the department conceded that if Cedarville College were a parochial school, it would not need such an endowment, for the weekly base of its constituency was regular and solid. This observation gave James an idea. "Well, why can't we use the offerings from our churches as a constituency base as the Catholics do?" The answer came back with a hiss. "You have no such base!" The state wanted nothing to do with James or his struggling college. The tone of the meeting made James feel as though the state not only would not help but that it would prefer the college to disappear. The hour drive home was long and tedious and filled with fear and doubt. *How is it possible, Lord, to pull the school out of the abyss when every turn seems to lead right back there again?* wondered James. If he were a Ph.D. from Harvard, the state would come to him. But he had no academic credentials, nothing to show for growth, nothing. But this attitude, so unfamiliar to James throughout his career, soon fell away. In its place came another plan. This time he would drive to neighboring Wittenberg University in Springfield.

Wittenberg University was a well-established liberal arts institution with a reputation for excellence. James sat down in the president's office, surrounded by large bookcases filled with old brown books. Before him sat the president of the university, older, looking very pristine in his bow tie and tweed jacket. He smiled at James warmly.

"I was president of a school just like Cedarville," said the man with a knowing look of empathy. "Back east, it was. It really went places . . . good school."

"Well," James replied, bolstered by those comments and the nostalgic look on the old man's face. "I am coming to ask you a favor. Would you help us? Would your people take our credits as though coming from an accredited school?" Suddenly, the old man's face soured, as though he had just imbibed a fly. His demeanor became intimidating and angry.

"No sir!" he boomed back. "You are never going to make it!" James realized that he had been fooled into believing that this pompous man was friendly. He gathered up his courage and shot back.

"Well now, *you* did."

"I was a young man then," replied the president, bow

tie drooping as though it, too, were frowning at James.

"I am a young man *now*," responded James as he stood to leave. And he walked out of the office.

James would remark, looking back upon that time much later, "I wish I could find that old guy. It's an awful carnal thing, but I wish I could find him and tell him, 'I have more students than you have.' That is carnal, and I would never do it; but it's fun, big fun, to think about sometimes."

The one thing that James could do was shore up his Regular Baptist base. He soon was urging Regular Baptists to support not only Cedarville College but other approved schools of the Association. He reminded them that Baptist schools needed their money and recognition and the prestige needed in the academic community.[14] He believed wholeheartedly that if the Association could lend monetary and advertising support, then at least the school could swim among its own. And as that belief started to be realized, the demand of immediate needs began to tax James' time.

Most presidents of small liberal arts colleges sit behind mahogany desks and spend their days in committee meetings discussing future plans and fiscal responsibilities. James, on the other hand, found himself making cement blocks for new construction and even "driving to Springfield to Reiter Dairy to pick up milk for the cafeteria."[15] And this type of willingness was what James brought to his new position. If it had to be done, he would personally see to it. The college was small enough at the time for this strategy to be effective. His philosophy was the opposite of the one reflected by most academics in the academic world who saw academia as an ivory tower, and who had a "let them eat cake" mentality.

This philosophy of doing "whatever it takes" had its drawbacks as well, for the college was having a hard time finding dedicated, quality faculty members who were willing to make below-average pay, put in long hours, and receive little immediate results for their efforts. The college was in such dire straits in the beginning that James, when away from the campus, "would call back and ask Ruby if there were enough money to pay the bills. 'She would go to the office and find out if we could pay salaries, and we always tried to get the faculty and staff salaries paid.' "[16] When payday came and money was tight, James would pay out what was owed, and only then would he pay himself. "The first summer after becoming president . . . [James] went six weeks without a salary."[17]

But God was blessing the small college and its president. When money was needed, it came in; when faculty positions were vacated, other faculty arrived to fill them. Life at the institution was progressing, and students were coming. By 1957 James had arranged a deal with Dayton's Wright-Patterson Air Force Base to buy two government housing units "120 feet long and 25 feet wide . . . at a token price of $25," to which James noted, "The expenditure is as great as that of larger colleges which must spend hundreds of thousands for building programs."[18] While this was not necessarily so, it shows how emphatic James was in comparing Cedarville College to any other bona fide college in academia. Faith Hall, as the building was named, soon was filled to capacity. God was slowly and steadily allowing the college to struggle along. Just as our Lord pulled from a small sack lunch some loaves and fish to feed the five thousand, He graciously allowed the college to sustain itself.

And James was also emphatic in making the college hold its ground against the prevailing liberalism of the day. The students and faculty of the young college would meet once a day for one hour to fellowship, to praise God, to communicate the gospel, and to keep the students and faculty abreast of the latest happenings. The chapel time was the most important time of the day, for it was at this moment that academics and social plans could be placed aside and complete focus could be given to the One Who allowed the college to exist.

Presently James decided to seek out the president of Central State College, the only Black state-funded institution in Ohio. Cedarville was still having major problems getting any of its educational programs accepted by state-run organizations, and Central State was James' last hope for a solution to that problem. The president's name was Dr. Charles Wesley.

"I said to him, 'Charles Wesley? With a name like that a man ought to be a Methodist.' " Wesley smiled knowingly and replied, "I am, but first and foremost I am a Christian." And the two men laughed out loud. "That fellow did everything he could to help us," remembers James. Dr. Wesley decided that Cedarville College "would give the content courses in education. 'And we will transfer those credits here, and we will give them credits and courses that the state demands. Then we will graduate them, and they will come back to Cedarville and you can graduate them.' " Charles Wesley also encouraged James to attend Central State to further his education, so James began his bachelor's degree at the age of forty-eight on a track to complete a major in history. James drove down to Central State, only about ten miles away, and spoke with an academic counselor.

The counselor welcomed him aboard and then got down to the business of arranging his schedule. He would be taking classes during the day, driving back and forth from his job as president over students to being a student himself. The counselor asked him if he had any language background to fulfill the requirements. James responded, "French." The counselor then told him that all he needed was one more class in that field. James put up his hands in defense: no, no, no. The last time he had spoken French was in high school at Johnson City! It was decided that he would take Spanish instead.

This decision, this taking classes at Central State College, an all-Black state-funded institution, is paramount in understanding one of the greatest events in James' life. In an age when segregation was still practiced, here was a Caucasian placing himself in a Black institution. It is also important to understand that the people of the late 1950s and 1960s took much of their culture for granted. We are often trapped in our own time, our own culture's prejudices. It is only when we look back with God's gift of time that we see our errors.

Many people did not want Blacks involved with Cedarville College, people as high up in the church as deacons and even leaders in the General Association of Regular Baptist Churches. "When I left that church in Dayton, a deacon said to me, 'If you take Blacks into that school, my daughter will never come.' And you know what I told him? Nothing. I just brought in Black students. And his daughter did come to the school, and she eventually married a Black man." James made a conscious decision not only to attend Central State College, but also to allow his college to participate with (via the education link) and, in a sense, to graduate from that university as well.

One day James was sitting in his Spanish class at Central State. His professor—a large jovial man with a nice disposition—was lumbering around the room asking different students questions in Spanish. He suddenly turned to James. "I don't know what he asked me, but I do remember that after I responded, he broke out in laughter. You see, I had answered in French, not Spanish."

Even toward the end of 1959, Cedarville was by no means out of its quandary, but the future was looking far brighter than it had when James inherited the situation of 1953. The faculty base was weak, numbering only 15, and the freshman class had only incrementally increased each year. In 1959 James wrote to the State of Ohio's Department

The Reluctant President

of Education for accreditation and boasted that "by 1970 we could care for between 600 and 700 students." Astoundingly his projection became reality far sooner than he or anyone else had expected. The *Xenia Gazette's* headline reported on August 3, 1963: "Cedarville College Expects 500 Pupils." As was the case in Panama, New York, as with Toledo and Dayton, God was moving and using James as His instrument.

As the academic year wound down, James finished his undergraduate studies at Central State College. On the last day of his Spanish class, the last class before finals, the large burly professor pulled James aside and explained that he need not bother coming in for the exam, that his grade was such that he had passed without any problem. The professor explained that he thought James had more important things to do than sit for an exam. The two shook hands, and James drove back to Cedarville. The day for the exam came and went, and he gave it no thought whatsoever.

Late one evening the following week, James heard a knock on his front door. He opened it, and to his complete surprise there stood his Spanish professor! James bid him come in. The large man looked sheepish. The two men sat down in the living room.

"James, we have a problem," explained the professor shaking his head. "It appears that when the other students found out that I exempted you from the final exam, several of them became upset. It appears that they are taking the matter to the academic dean for further consideration. Apparently they think I showed favoritism to you because of your skin color." James was aghast. He realized the position that this good man was in and wanted to do anything he could to make it right.

"What can I do?" he asked his professor and friend.

"Well," replied the man as he repositioned himself on the couch, reaching over to his briefcase and pulling several items from it, "here is the book. And here is the exam. Take the test, hand it in to me, and you will hear no more of this." James showed the man out, took the test, and never did hear from him again.

In February 1960, the *Columbus Dispatch* reported:

> The dean's list of Central State College has a lot of class—it contains the name of a college president. Among the 67 honor students on the list is the Rev. James T. Jeremiah, president of Cedarville College in Cedarville, Ohio. To be included on the dean's list, a student must make an average of 3.2 or better. Mr. Jeremiah, history major, made it with a 3.21 average.[19]

While this publicity seems friendly, the coverage and number of newspapers that mentioned this graduate posed a risk. It was most peculiar indeed that a president of a college would be graduating from another institution with a degree that his own college granted. And here is where the subtle attacks from those headlines came into play. Most institutions around the area were probably looking upon Cedarville College as a backward, truly nonacademic institution. If the president of the college did not even have a bachelor's degree, what must the college be like? And even more so, the comment regarding his GPA seemed quite harmless on the surface and seemed even like a plug. But when the article compared the criteria for admission to the dean's list and James' GPA, a wary reader would catch on that the president of the college had just barely made the list. Indeed, he had made it by one point.

That James did acquire his bachelor's degree was a significant step for him personally. A nonacademic youth called to be a pastor (not a scholar) did not need a college degree, let alone an advanced degree. But after he found himself in the academic community with no degree at all, he had decided to lead by example.

The Reluctant President

The same year that James graduated, Dr. Charles Wesley, president of Central State College, gave an address at Cedarville in commemoration of a new fifty-room dormitory, which housed one hundred students.[20] Dr. Wesley joined Joseph Stowell, then pastor of First Baptist Church in Hackensack, New Jersey, in speaking highly of the progress of the college and the leadership and vision of its president.

The following year, President Wesley reciprocated the honor by having James Jeremiah give the baccalaureate address to the "class of 1961 Sunday at 10:00 A.M. in Galloway Chapel on the campus at Wilberforce."[21] During the graduation ceremony Dr. Wesley honored James further with an honorary doctor of divinity degree in recognition of his contributions in the fields of religion and education. James Jeremiah had now become Dr. Jeremiah, and a relationship and friendship forged over several years had now benefited both institutions and both men.

Early in 1959 James had addressed the graduating high school class at Cedarville High School with these words:

> There ought to be in this life a degree of
> sincerity and not one of sham and pretense.
> We need a sense of responsibility that no
> matter what our task may be, we are dedicated
> to what we are doing."[22]

James had lived out those statements by forging a relationship with Central State College and with its president. In actions and not in words, in a time when Blacks and whites were on the verge of physical violence toward each other, James Jeremiah showed how Christ, not politics, binds brothers to one another. In just two years James had crossed a racial divide that would take the United States a decade or more to cross. But the tumultuous '60s had begun, and Cedarville College was not immune from the terrible repercussions it would inflict.

ENDNOTES

1. All quotations of James T. Jeremiah, unless otherwise stated, are taken from personal interviews conducted by the author.
2. J. Murray Murdoch, *Cedarville College: A Century of Commitment* (Cedarville, Ohio: Cedarville College, 1987), 105.
3. Ibid., 106.
4. Ibid., 108.
5. Dayton, Ohio. Emmanuel Baptist Church. Dedication of new building. 21 March 1954, church bulletin.
6. Murdoch, 106, 107.
7. Ibid., 107.
8. Ibid., 108.
9. Ibid.
10. Ibid.
11. *The Ohio Independent Baptist*, 10 October 1954.
12. Murdoch, 116.
13. Ibid., 118.
14. Ibid., 114.
15. Ibid., 108.
16. Ibid., 109.
17. Ibid.
18. *Dayton Journal Herald*, 20 September 1957.
19. *Columbus Dispatch*, 27 February 1960.
20. *Dayton Journal Herald*, 8 October 1960.
21. *Xenia Gazette*, 31 May 1961.
22. *Springfield News-Sun*, May 24, 1959.

Chapter 5

Raising the Dead
(1962–1970)

Societal change during the 1960s was so dramatic that no institution or individual was unaffected. The conscience of the country was shaken at times by violence and at other times by peaceful protest. The elderly longed for the days of the past, of simple, tangible times; for the world was again rapidly changing, fast becoming unrecognizable to the World War II generation. Drug-taking, sexually loose young adults seized the opportunity to trash all ties with the present. For some it was a moment to change the world, to incite revolution. But for most it was like boarding a roller coaster—climbing and swooping through technological, social, and political upheaval.

James Jeremiah had successfully guided Cedarville College out of the uncertainty of its new beginning, but great changes still had to take place if the college were to be truly accepted in the world of higher education. Accreditation by the state would solve that problem. What needed to be done was quite apparent. How it was to be done, however, was befuddling to James. He had successfully managed to forge strong ties with the General Association of Regular Baptist Churches, which ultimately became the fundamental base for Cedarville's student body and its conservative views. But the academic world did not understand or even care to understand religious-based education.

They wanted certification, a mandate by the state.

The Jeremiah family had settled into their new home and new way of life. Soon the college consumed their lives. Ruby, especially, became immersed in the new push of advertisement and promotion, things James had always advocated. If the school were going to survive, it would need much publicity. Along with speaking at as many Regular Baptist churches as possible, James began to make the necessary contacts. But a need soon became apparent—the need for something to give his audiences, something to put in their hands. It was Ruby's idea to begin printing brochures and pamphlets. "Personnel was scarce. [Ruby] soon found herself working part-time in the mail room. . . . And when the school needed some means of printing its own literature, she learned to work an offset press."[1] The college was not keen on the idea of purchasing the printer; the board loathed to spend the money frivolously. So James bought the machine himself and placed it in his basement. Ruby learned how to use it, and they started the first of thousands of campaigns to raise money. As these methods proved effective, the board of trustees realized the importance the press played along with James' speaking engagements, and they purchased the machine, giving it a space on campus. Each day Ruby would venture into the basement of the old administration building, turn on the printer, and begin the process; soon afterwards "both apron and face [were] streaked with printer's ink."[2] By 1964 Ruby had the printing down to a science and was printing "38,000 bulletins compared to her first run of 3,700."[3] She would tell a reporter one day, "I'm still not quite sure why I learned to do this, but we're hoping to hire someone to do this work full-time[;] it has grown so much."[4]

The Jeremiah children were also growing up rapidly. In the mid-1960s, two had already moved out of the house, and two still lived in Cedarville. Loisanne married David

Mills and moved to Grand Rapids, Michigan. David had graduated from Cedarville College and was attending Dallas Theological Seminary. Maryalyce, a senior at the college, was studying physical education, and sixteen-year-old Jim was a junior at the local high school.[5] The children had decided to attend the local high school. Although the school was small, the Jeremiah children believed that supporting the college and the community was a good idea. James and Ruby had offered to drive them to some other secondary school, one with more sports programs, but the vote was unanimous.

Ruby didn't mind working hand in hand with James: "I feel it is my responsibility to help my husband, and besides he does not like to travel alone, and I do not like to stay home alone."[6] But the toll of such effort had a price. Ruby felt the barbs of those who disapproved of her working in the print shop, acting as part of the Maintenance Department when she should have been acting as a "first lady" of the college. "You are very open to criticism and the views of people who do not agree with your methods," she remarked. "It is even harder on children, I think, because young people can be so cruel without meaning to be. But ours have accepted it quite well."[7] As time went on, the college hired someone else to run the printer, and Ruby was able to stay at home.

One day, just before he was to speak in chapel, James received a phone call. His father, Thomas Jeremiah, was in the hospital in serious condition.

The influences of a father on a child are great—for good or bad. "Children are likely to imitate what they see in their fathers," wrote James in a book on the Christian home. "Dads, you are one of the most important blocks in the battlement around your home. If you are not in the proper position in the spiritual wall, your children will fall to their harm and your sorrow. The priority in your life is being the best husband and father you can be by the grace of God and for the good of your children."[8]

And Thomas Jeremiah had done the best he could for Flora, James, and Edward. Several times James had visited his father, who was still living in Johnson City with Flora. Thomas, old and withered by the hard work in his life, was skinny, with a chiseled jaw.

Thomas Jeremiah did not attend church. James bought him a Bible and talked to him about the Lord but received little response.

"One day I said, 'You know, Dad, to go off into eternity without Christ as your Savior . . . that is terrible.' He said something to the effect of, 'A man would have to be foolish to do that.' "[9]

But even after that conversation James was not sure of his father's position on eternal issues. He thought that "somewhere along the line, someone had talked to him" about Jesus. "One teacher where Dad worked was a member of a good fundamentalist church. And this lady would talk to him."

But "it was hard to get any commitment from Dad. He had had a hard life, and I can't explain it. My heart aches because I am not sure. But God knows."

"God will hear a believing parent's prayer of intercession for a son or daughter just as He hears the child's petition in behalf of a prodigal mother or a wayward father."[10]

Knowing that his father was in the hospital, James called his mother, stating that he wished to visit his dad there. Flora told her son to wait until Thomas came home. "Well, he never came home. He died right there in the hospital." Thomas Jeremiah was dead of a heart attack at the age of seventy-nine.

It so happened that the man who held his funeral services was the very same one who had married Flora and Thomas so many years earlier. On his way back to the college from the funeral, James kept remembering his father's silliest traits. An image popped into his head: his father is working in the yard when suddenly and without warning a car zooms by going about sixty miles an hour, and Thomas becomes furious. "That would upset him for about the entire day."

* * *

Earlier in 1962, James made his first move to place around him a team of people who could effectively pull the school up from its academic quagmire. Thanks to James' efforts with Regular Baptist churches, very strong financial support was coming in. But the state was still unwilling to accommodate the college. That was when James called Dr. Cliff Johnson, an elementary school principal from the State of Washington, to be the college's registrar. Bringing Johnson on board was the first prong in a four-pronged attack set in motion by James.

Johnson was soon in charge of creating an Education Department that would pass the state's requirements. On his first visit to the superintendent of public instruction, however, he was in for a rude awakening. "I got chewed out for about ten minutes, but I just tried to keep my cool. When he was all done, I asked him if he would be willing to help us do what needed to be done."[11] This request prompted a visit by the assistant superintendent of public instruction, and soon Dr. Johnson had his hands full of regulations and requirements to pass the next inspection. These rapidly passed muster, and by 1963 Cedarville College could offer classes in education and, by 1967, grant degrees.

This move by Dr. Johnson and the State of Ohio elated James, and he pronounced the occasion as "one of the big days in the short history of Cedarville College. . . . [It] brings to life a ten-year dream. . . . We are extremely happy that at last we can begin work toward turning out teachers. That's been our big goal ever since our denomination took over the college."[12] Now the college could offer degrees that could be accepted anywhere in the State of Ohio. Reaching this goal meant that James' special connection with Central State College and with his good friend Charles Wesley was over. James publicly expressed that "while his school [would] terminate a cooperative program with nearby Central State College in the field of education, Cedarville graduates with bachelor's degrees [would] still seek master's degrees at CSC."[13]

Attaining this milestone was a jubilant, thankful occasion for James. He knew how much his friend at Central State had helped convince the State of Ohio that Cedarville College was worthy of its approval. James' oldest daughter Loisanne, and hundreds of others as well, had graduated from that cooperative program. The first peg in a long line of pegs was finally in place. The next step was to move the college toward a visit from the North Central Association accreditation team and finally full accreditation and the final stamp of approval by the State of Ohio.

The second prong of James' four-prong attack was Kenneth H. St. Clair, whose main job was to create and set in motion all the necessary elements for a dynamic Business Department. St. Clair soon started the program that "was to develop into Cedarville's largest major."[14] The third prong of James' attack was Richard McIntosh, who became Dean of Students. McIntosh was in charge of improving the institution's facilities for student services. "During his tenure, [he] expanded campus health services and established the Financial Aid Department."[15] But it was the fourth and final prong that set Cedarville on a firm foundation. James knew the essentiality of giving, of monetary support and, with it, advertisement and promotion. It was with this essential in mind that he hired the last of his "four horsemen," Lee C. Turner. Turner soon laid the foundation for programs that would be used throughout the history of the college, programs such as planned giving and The President's Association. He also created *The Torch* magazine, which promoted the college and informed the alumni of new developments and new visions.

The hiring of these four men was the first of two major events that characterized James as a leader and a college president. The second would come much later, as his days as president were coming to an end.

These four men became dynamic, innovative personnel who made key decisions and really set the college on track. James would concede later that had it not been for those four men, the college would not have made it. Having such movers and shakers in place allowed James to travel often and regularly and to speak against the heresies of the day, against those who were resistant toward Christian education, and concerning those who found themselves lost in a world of anarchy, a world reeling from the blows of a rebellious, defiant generation.

At about that time, James began what he had started all the way back in Toledo: a radio program. Since the school was just pulling out of its financial crisis, beginning such an expensive proposition as a radio station was risky. Some faculty members disagreed with James' decision.

> One faculty member said it wouldn't work, that we didn't have the money. Most people did not understand the concept of reaching people on the radio. I had a desire to use it as a means of getting the gospel out. That was my main objective. And I always believed if you do what God tells you to do, He honors it. He honored that radio station. I didn't argue with the faculty member and just said, "We'll try. We'll try." The radio has helped so many people.

And that radio station did fly; it did stay off the ground; its waves scattered across Ohio and beyond. David Jeremiah and Paul Gathany were the first two students to broadcast from WCDR in Cedarville College. "On December 1, 1962, [they] began broadcasting. . . . The first program was a live play-by-play broadcast of a basketball game between Grace College and Cedarville in Winona Lake, Indiana."[16] This radio outlet would become an important vehicle for James to broadcast his messages of hope in the tumultuous days of the next two decades.

"A rebel," explained James as he spoke into the microphone of WCDR, "is one who resists or defies any authority or generally accepted ruling authority. The 'authority' may be the government, the home, the school, church, or place of employment. [Rebellion], if unchecked, will grow and in many cases has grown [into] civil disobedience and crime. . . . [It] has not been checked but tolerated in almost every area of life."[17] And as he looked across his nation, James became more and more distraught with the problems on other university campuses. "Our generation has been characterized by rebellion and dissent—there have been sit-ins, bombings, lockouts, protests, demands, campouts, marches, and parades of one sort or another."[18] But he knew that the rebellion and riots were nothing more than "another symptom of our sin-sick society, . . . breeding a generation of criminals who fear neither God nor man."[19] As his message ended, James pleaded with his audience that one should not look at the confusion and chaos, but focus on the message: "God wants His people to submit to Him and the authority of His Word. When Christians do that, they will be the law-abiding citizens they are expected to be."[20]

James also had views on modesty, a key factor in the Regular Baptist makeup. "The Word of God teaches that men and women should be clothed. A hairy-chested, barefoot, undressed man is hardly a walking expression of beauty."[21] But Cedarville College was not the norm during those riotous days of the '60s. In fact, a large Dayton paper's headline read, "At Cedarville, Happiness Is Not a Mini-Skirt." James retorted to the reporter, who obviously sought a loaded interview, "They are Christian kids, and that makes all the difference. We have some regulations here, and we enforce them, but we don't ask the young people to live outside their generation either."[22]

But growing pains were developing throughout the college, tension points between James and his faculty that were bound to erupt. James was a man of conviction, deeply instilled in him from his days at Baptist Bible Seminary in Johnson City, New York. He had no tolerance for those who would not catch his vision or that of his four administrators. Cedarville College, although growing, was no larger than a medium-sized high school. James was not so much a president as a "father figure to a lot of the faculty as well as to a lot of the students."[23] And this father treated his campus accordingly. "At times he treated [faculty] like naughty children. And yet at the same time there was a kind of curiosity about him. There were areas where he was really locked in, and other areas where he was not sure."[24]

During one occasion several ambitious faculty members wished to start a restaurant on a corner lot near the college. James came down upon the idea like thunder. In essence, he demanded that they give all their attention to the college and to their profession. If they chose to run a restaurant, then that was what they should do, not teach at the college. "The Big Wheel" incident became a hot button between James and his faculty, for the average pay at that time was a mere $6,000. James "gave 14, 16, 20 hours a day to the school."[25] Those who tried to make extra money or place themselves in outside ministries other than the college were soon reprimanded. One faculty member had become an interim pastor. His little church had been booming, and he was trying to "bring things together. The church had gone from 30 to 150 members."[26] James got wind of the interim pastorate and the fact that the professor had changed his membership to the church he was leading. He soon showed up at the man's office. "You've got thirty days, and you are out of there," declared James. "You are either going to be a pastor, or you are going to work here. As far as I am concerned you have a contract with us, and you need to honor it."[27]

Months later James called the faculty member into his office. "Whatever happened to that church you were in up there?" he asked good-naturedly.

"You don't want to know what I think happened."

James looked puzzled and concerned.

"Yes I do, brother," he replied.

"No, you don't," repeated the faculty member.

"Yes," continued James, a little bit impatient with his employee. "Yes, I want to know."

The faculty member looked him in the eye and stated, "Doc, I think what happened is a classic example of what happens when man moves a man instead of God moving a man."

After that statement, "the sparks just flew across the desk. [The professor] thought [James] was going to can him right on the spot." But then James gathered himself together, checked his temper, "looked down for a bit, let the fire go and then looked back up and said, 'Brother, I hope you are wrong.' "[28]

There were times to be dogmatic, and there were times to be conciliatory. James had learned early in his pastorate that to get something done, he had to do it himself. But one could not operate that way with faculty or scholars. They had their ways, their bents. When it came to issues of the school, perhaps James swept more widely than he should have. His ambition and focus were single-minded: Cedarville College. A divided faculty is an impotent one. He knew that if a professor were to carry out two jobs, neither one would come to any good. He knew this result firsthand, for it had been as a pastor in Dayton that he had been forced to divide his time between his congregation and a dying college. The stresses and strains from that time lingered far longer than his career. Perhaps he swung the gavel too fast, too harshly, but experience had taught him that God uses one completely and wholly, never part-time and never just a little. And when there were incidents like that one with the faculty member/pastor, Dr. Johnson would usually be the one to step in and mediate, blunting the rough edges of James' demands.

But at other moments in the history of the college, James stood firm, for he was convinced that the college's stand on doctrinal issues would either destroy or establish the college. His moment of truth was coming, and he would have to cut severely and deeply if the institution's integrity were to survive.

Professors were beginning to discuss among themselves a theory known as the Day-Age and how it held up against the literal six-day view of creation. The Day-Age theory purports that instead of seven twenty-four-hour days, God created the world in ages or huge expanses of time. This theory supposedly supported evidence that was being discovered by the scientific community: layers of strata dating millions of years into the past. The conversations were really being instigated by a few faculty members: one in the Biology Department, another in the Business Department, and one in the Music Department. Soon the campus buzzed with professors taking sides, with grumblings and murmurings of resignation.

James became concerned as the rumors and innuendoes surfaced. His stance was definitive: "The Day-Age theory is nothing more than disguised evolution. That is what it is. And if God couldn't have made the earth in six days, then He couldn't have made it in six centuries." The problem became so divisive that James called the board together to discuss the issue and commit to one side or the other. Division is always wrong in any institution, whether a church or a college, and James knew that if this debate lasted, it would cut into the cohesiveness of his faculty. If the faculty members were not on the same page, wholly committed to the furthering of the college, then the student body would suffer. "I am more concerned about biology teachers than I am of philosophy teachers; they interject science and humanism as if it were truth."

So the board decided to meet, to hash out the position that the school would abide by, and to settle the dissention once and for all. A certain professor began "popping off." "If the board of trustees decides for other than the Day-Age theory, then I am leaving, I am leaving, I am leaving,' he proclaimed." And there were others as well. In fact, the Day-Age theory had captured the fancy of a significant number of faculty members and more than a few stalwart, reputable professors.

The board of trustees met over the weekend in secret, unbeknown to the faculty, and the meeting lasted all day. By evening they had decided that Cedarville College would abide by the literal twenty-four-hour-day view of creation. That night James printed a letter with the doctrinal statement and position that the college would take and placed it in all faculty and staff mailboxes. When Monday arrived, all the faculty were apprised of the new position:

> The college now upholds the theory that the seven days of creation recorded in Genesis are in fact literal solar days. Those who hold a position contrary to the solar day may not serve as a Trustee, in the administration, or on the faculty.[29]

The shock was overwhelming. Even those who did not agree with the Day-Age theory were upset with the way the board had handled the matter. And the grumblings continued. "I heard that one professor said, 'If I were president, I would have done it differently.' So," recalled James years later, "I invited him into my office and offered him the job." There was silence, and the professor turned away defeated and humbled. "I wanted to win. I had to at that point."

James remembered the grumblings of the one professor who had proclaimed his resignation if the board decided against the Day-Age theory. He called the man to his office. "I wanted to bring you in here because I want to tell you something: how much I admire you. You are a man of your word. You have been telling everybody that if we did this, you were going to leave. Well, it is done; now what are you going to do?"

"That's what I will have to do then," replied the professor. With no way out, he packed and left.

"I had no alternative. I made up my mind I was not going to be president any longer if I had to put up with 'I will leave, I will leave, I will leave.' That kind of talk sows discord. If we were to go the way of evolution, brother, we would have been through." And three months later, in big bold headlines, a local paper pronounced: "Four Cedarville Profs Leave."[30] In a complete affront against the college and its decision to uphold the literal six-day creation, the paper made sure to add, "Those leaving include [name], professor of biology and one of only three Ph.D.s on the faculty."[31] This barb unmistakably showed the bias of the writer, who in effect was saying, "If these professors are leaving, one even a Ph.D., then, dear reader, you know how backward and unenlightened the school must be." James came down heavy because his convictions on the subject were so strong. He knew that God, not he, was moving the school forward and that if he were to give in to what he did not believe, he had no business governing that academic body. The school took several months to overcome the blow that this stir created. One of the local papers sought out students to interview. Several responded without giving their names. The reporter stated:

> Widespread student dissatisfaction with the Trustees' ruling has been reported, but students refuse to be quoted as they might be subject to disciplinary action. The action has been discussed in faculty, Student Council and other meetings recently and has been raised in the daily chapel programs, it is said.[32]

James was receiving blow after blow from without and within. He knew how to deal with dissenters: either you are for us, or you are against us. But earlier, before the Day-Age controversy, he had received another severe blow, this time by the State of Ohio. He needed Cedarville to pass a review by the North Central Association of Colleges and Secondary Schools to become established in the eyes of other academic institutions. Dr. Johnson had done a splendid job in convincing the board to visit the campus. By December 1964, the North Central committee had visited, and by April their review had come in. James and Cliff Johnson traveled to Chicago for the answer: Cedarville was still too unstable for the committee's liking. "Cedarville was asked to continue to study its program in the areas of financial stability, completion of the new $300,000 library, and increasing the number of people holding graduate degrees at the college."[33] The final peg was not yet in place, and James could do nothing to make it happen. He had to once again wait upon the Lord and His leading. At this time James was being attacked on still another front. Bob Jones University, specifically Bob Jones himself, was berating the college for giving into the whole idea of accreditation by the state. James was furious but did not respond to the rambunctious letters sent from the institution. He had a theory, and time proved it: Let them yell all they want. It's publicity for us, and it's free.

Raising the Dead

After chapel on May 21, 1965, James received a letter. He opened it and read: "Dad, I heard chapel. Congratulations. No one deserves it more. From your #2 daughter." He closed the letter and smiled. During that day's chapel, the student body had made a presentation: they had decided to dedicate the 1965 yearbook to their president, James T. Jeremiah. It had been a rough year, and the following years would be rougher, but through it all Cedarville College was establishing itself as a leader in Christian education.

"Our young people are becoming brainwashed by this godless society." James was on another promotional tour, speaking to churches. "This should be sufficient reason why every thinking Christian parent should be interested in Christian education." He had been on a weekend trip to several GARBC churches, and his mission was to hammer one point home:

> If we intend to keep our young people within "the biblical battlement" of our home, we must provide for them an education that is Christian. The teaching schedule must begin in infancy and continue through the years of higher education. Therefore, we must build and support Christian schools.[34]

James had understood the arguments for and against Christian education long ago. He had seen firsthand the destruction to the faith that other institutions promoted. And he knew what some Christians were thinking about the subject. He attacked the fallacies ruthlessly, cutting them apart like a surgeon, each in a logical fashion. One of the biggest arguments purported by the opposition was isolationism:

> Is this to say [in response to the argument of isolationism] that we should care less for our children than we do for some fragile plant? If we possessed a very rare flower and desired to see it grow and blossom, would we protect it in a hothouse or put it outdoors in sub-zero

> weather? The answer is obvious. Our Christian young people need to be taught, protected, and prepared to live and serve Christ in this world that desperately needs the Savior. Our Christian youth generally will be better prepared if educated in Christian schools.[35]

The real crux of his efforts, however, was not only to promote Christian education, but to move the audience to support Cedarville College, an institution that was doing all that he claimed Christian education should do:

> Perhaps you argue that it is much cheaper to send your children to a secular college and save money for missionary endeavors so that the heathen can be converted. Are you really more concerned about the pagan across the sea than you are about your own children when you willingly subject them to intellectual pagans for their education? It is time some Christian parents gave greater consideration to the importance of Christian education.[36]

It was not enough for parents to acknowledge the concept of Christian education, but to act accordingly, to respond where it affected them the most—the pocketbook:

> If our young people are to enjoy the privileges of Christian education from their early years through the experience of higher education, then Christian people must sacrificially support Christian schools. No one of us can excuse himself from this responsibility.[37]

On April 4, 1968, in a hotel in Memphis, Tennessee, a shot rang out, and Martin Luther King Jr., was gunned down. Hearing about the event on the television, James immediately picked up the phone. The professor on the other end answered, "Hello."

"What are you doing?" boomed James.

"I'm just sitting here, watching television and taking it all in." The history professor had driven the Cedarville

College tennis team to Kentucky and was about to travel to Nashville for a tournament. James interrupted him.

"You are not going to Nashville."

"No," responded the professor, "I'm planning on calling the coach down there in a little bit, but my plan is to spend the day here."

"Well," replied James sternly and concernedly, "don't even think about going down there. . . ." James hesitated and then made his point exceptionally clear: "What I'm telling you is you are not going to Nashville." That response stuck with the professor, for years later he would recall,

> Here it was that we were small enough that the president of the school catches this [news report], and . . . realizes that I've got a group from [our] college that's on [its] way down into [the situation], and this is not going to be real safe. [So] he was on the phone at six o'clock to make sure we did not get involved in anything difficult.[38]

James had little toleration for bigots, and the murder of Martin Luther King Jr., underscored his deep convictions:

> In more recent times and in our own country, white people have detested, mistreated, and downgraded blacks. The blacks have hated, despised, and fought the whites. In some instances there seems to be no thought of equality on either side of the conflict. Racism reigns to our utter shame and should be stopped. In our opinion, only Christ in the hearts of believing sinners can change the direction we are going.[39]

When James was sure about his convictions, when he knew that a Biblical mandate supported his position, he could not be swayed off course. However, in those areas where room for interpretation existed, he usually was generally inquisitive and open minded. During several heated conversations over interracial marriages and the mixing of Blacks and whites, and after much Biblical study, James concluded that "there [is] more in the Bible against Christians marrying non-Christians. . . ." He stated emphatically, "It is our opinion that there is no Bible verse that states interracial marriages are unscriptural. On the other hand, there are good reasons to believe they are generally unwise."[40]

James did concede in the areas that he was unsure of. He would frequently call in faculty members and ask, "Brother, what do you think about this? What do you think about that?" At one point rumors were flying concerning a church in Michigan whose pastor was casting out demons in Christians. Some of the professors had voiced interest in the topic. James called in a trusted friend, a history professor, one who would shoot straight with him. He motioned for him to sit down. James had a look of concern, as though a serious burden lay across his brow.

"Brother," said James gruffly, "what do you think of this business casting demons out of Christians?"

The professor looked quite serious as well. Their eyes met.

"Frankly, Jim, it scares the Devil out of me." James looked at his friend sternly, a serious demeanor still covering his face, and then he began to shake with laughter.[41]

Toward the end of that decade, the college was beginning to blossom into an institution that could pull its weight and provide a fundamental Christian education coupled with a Biblically based liberal arts approach. It had weathered several major storms from within and without. The college now had a good financial standing, and the faculty was stable and academically sound. And even the community of Cedarville was benefiting from the exposure to the college. The wary townspeople for the first time looked favorably at a man and an institution that had at one time seemingly mocked them. On September 10, 1969, James presented a check of $1,000 to the village in "appreciation for the services the village makes available to [the college]. In a letter with the check, [James] wrote that the college desired the best possible relationship with the community and [that the college family would] do all [it could] to help [the village] in any way."[42]

James was entering his fifty-fifth year. His kids had grown and gone: David was becoming a successful pastor with a radio broadcast all his own; Loisanne was married and living in Tennessee; Maryalyce was working in academia; and Jim was married and had children. Furthermore, Ruby was in good spirits, happy as a mother and a "first lady." James could look back on a decade and a half of God's blessings. "It all comes down to one thing, brother. It is so amazing that it could not be human. It had to be God. You talk about raising the dead? Nobody knows that better than I do."

ENDNOTES

1. "First Lady of Cedarville," *Dayton Daily News*, 25 October 1964.
2. Ibid.
3. Ibid.
4. Ibid.
5. Ibid.
6. Ibid.
7. Ibid.
8. James T. Jeremiah, *The House That Stands* (Cedarville, Ohio: Christian Educational Publications, 1974).
9. All quotations of James T. Jeremiah, unless otherwise noted, are taken from interviews conducted by the author.
10. *The House That Stands*, 15.
11. J. Murray Murdoch, *Cedarville College: A Century of Commitment* (Cedarville, Ohio: Cedarville College, 1987), 125.
12. "Cedarville College Gets OK on Teacher Education Plan," *Xenia Daily Gazette*, 13 June 1963.
13. *Xenia Daily Gazette*, 19 June 1963.

14. Murdoch, 126.
15. Ibid.
16. Murdoch, 120.
17. James T. Jeremiah, *Questions People Are Asking* (Cedarville, Ohio: Cedarville College, 1979), 28.
18. Ibid., 29
19. Ibid.
20. Ibid.
21. Ibid, 36.
22. "At Cedarville, Happiness Is Not a Mini-Skirt," *Dayton Daily News*, 8 April 1968.
23. J. Murray Murdoch, personal interview, 6 April 1998.
24. Ibid.
25. Ibid.
26. Ibid.
27. Ibid.
28. Ibid.
29. "Cedarville College Takes Stand on Creation of Universe," *Dayton Daily News*, 17 January 1967.
30. "Four Cedarville Profs Leave," *Xenia Gazette*, 22 April 1967.
31. Ibid.
32. Ibid.
33. "North Central Turns Down Cedarville," *Daily Gazette*, 2 April 1965.
34. *The House That Stands*, 28.
35. Ibid., 29.
36. Ibid.
37. Ibid.
38. Murdoch, interview.
39. *Questions*, 76.
40. Ibid., 78.
41. Murdoch, interview.
42. *Xenia Gazette*, 10 September 1969.

Chapter 6

Your Finest Hour
(1971–1978)

Dear friends, my wife and I are looking forward to the fulfillment of a lifelong dream. On July 31 we plan to begin a fifteen-day tour of the Bible lands."[1] James and Ruby were excited. They had finally come to a place in their lives (and in the college's life) that a trip abroad was not only acceptable but warranted. This trip would be their first time out of the United States, and the letter written to those who would join them was filled with enthusiasm. "What a thrill it will be to visit some of the places Jesus walked and performed many of His miracles! This will truly be a trip of a lifetime."[2] They would leave from New York City and fly to Cairo to see the Great Pyramids; then to Beirut, Nazareth, the Dead Sea, Jerusalem, Athens, Corinth; and then back to New York. This tour would be the first of fifteen trips, nearly one every year.

James had always been fascinated with the lands of the Bible, especially as they related to the end times. This interest culminated in a booklet he had printed in 1974 titled *Converging Signs*. In that publication, James demonstrated how the world was groaning to an end, how the signs of the end of the age were coming together. He used his Biblical knowledge and his experiences in Jerusalem and abroad to illustrate the prophetic messages in the Bible and then used prophecy as a platform to call people to a saving belief in Christ.

When he returned from that first trip, the college was abuzz over something: North Central accreditation. The committee that had reviewed the campus in 1965 and had ultimately rejected the college's membership planned to return. With the help of his "four horsemen," James had established a credible institution. Since the last observation by the committee, the college had added a library and new faculty, had increased enrollment, and had raised substantial amounts of funds in the process. If the college could acquire accreditation from the committee, then every school in the area would have to accept Cedarville's credits. Preparations began, and the college readied itself for the visit.

On October 19, 1973, James and Ruby were honored at a banquet. The board of trustees had gathered the college family together to celebrate James and Ruby's contribution over the last twenty years. As speaker after speaker stood to express gratitude and praise, James began to remember all those years that had flowed under the bridge. God had moved in an undeniable way. His early days as country preacher going out into the fields to share the gospel with farmers and his pastorates in Toledo and Dayton—those days seemed a lifetime away, a hazy memory, someone else's life. And indeed, they almost were. For twenty years James and Ruby had shifted gears and had become something that neither of them ever expected: a college president and wife. The struggles with the dying school, the takeover, Webster, the many attacks by the enemy from all sides—all of this seemed distant now.

Cliff Johnson stood and extolled James' virtues as a leader, a father figure who was always there. And the rest of the "four horsemen" acknowledged, each in his turn, the impact that James and Ruby had had on their lives. Paul Gathany, now running the radio station, WCDR, expressed his gratitude for the vision of such a station at such a college, noting that the outreach broadcasted to hundreds of thousands across Ohio and to other places as well. The day was, indeed, a time of reflection, of tears, of gratitude. But James knew Who had caused all of the success, and he knew to Whom to give credit:

> I am astounded. I can't tell you how much, because I know that I couldn't have done it. I could not have done it. I've made stupid mistakes along the way, but the Lord overcame them. I don't know.... [I]t's beyond my understanding. I would rather have it that way than any other.[3]

James knew very well the pitfalls of education, and he knew if the college were to maintain its growth and quality, it must focus on the spiritual:

> We must never lose the emphasis on chapel, and we must never lose the preaching in chapel that has something to say about Christian living, salvation. Never. And if we do, we have lost the whole thing.

The colleges across the country that had failed, that had caved into the pressures of secularism had, in James' words, "tried to reach people by conforming to what people are instead of conforming to the way they ought to be." He continued,

> Their way, you don't know what you've got when you get it.... Those schools that have gone down that road have stopped having chapel. And that has done them in.

James and Ruby were deeply moved by the kind words and tribute, but the most thrilling part was yet to come. Toward the end of the speeches and acknowledgments, the board unveiled a portrait of James. The painting is distinguished: James in a dark suit, his completely white and thinning hair combed back, horned rimmed glasses bridging a confident brow. And then the board handed James and Ruby a set of keys to a twenty-foot motor home. They could travel in comfort and style, driving thousands of miles a year visiting churches and their children, who were now scattered across the country. It was a glorious evening, one that the two of them would hold dear the rest of their lives.

One day a reporter from a Dayton paper knocked on James' door.

"Come in," invited James, always obliging the press, for it provided free publicity.

"Say," sneered the reporter, "I hear that your college does not promote academic freedom." James looked down at his desk and then out the window, the sun now shining down prominently across the campus. He knew where the man was coming from; he knew that he was looking to trap him.

"Well," said James, smiling politely, "we do promote academic freedom. We teach evolution, . . ." he let that word drip off his tongue, all the while gauging the reporter's expression of shock and disbelief, ". . . paganism, and all the rest." The reporter began to scribble something on his notepad. And that was when James zapped him. "We teach what is wrong with them. We also have a Bible Department devoted solely to truth. Go to Ohio State University and see where their Bible Department is." James leaned back in his chair with another polite smile. The reporter had stopped writing. A long silence ensued, and then the reporter stood and walked out the door.

By November 1974 James and his faculty were ready for the North Central visit. "Every aspect of the college" was to be evaluated. "Students, faculty, staff, and administration were questioned. Records were checked. Library holdings were evaluated."[4] In essence, the committee combed through any tangent of the college that could be mismanaged or underdeveloped. When they left the campus, the college family exhaled an anxious sigh. But a report still had to be written and presented during the accrediting association's annual meeting. James and his confidant, Dr. Cliff Johnson, would be sure to attend.

One day James came out of his office in Founders Hall, pulled his keys from his pockets, and then froze; recovering, he silently shook his head. For quite some time, several of the students had been playing pranks on the campus. There in his parking place, instead of his car, stood a motorcycle—helmet on one handlebar, a backpack (completely stuffed) hanging on the back. James chuckled, for this vehicle presented an image of himself that he had never considered. Several days later he received through campus mail a picture of that very motorcycle with a wooden nameplate, "Dr. J. Jeremiah," quite visible in the background. This would be a picture to keep and show to Ruby.

But soon it was time to go to Chicago. James and Dr. Johnson drove to the city and found themselves waiting patiently as the committee met. It was not long until they were called before the group. It seems that before they cast the final votes, several of the members had some questions.

James sat down and greeted everyone. He was a bit nervous. Sure, he had been through such things before, but his dealings with the state had always been confrontational. Why should these matters be any different? He began to think of all the possible scenarios. The college just had to get this approval. So much was riding on it. Ice formed in his stomach as several members shuffled papers and asked what seemed to be irrelevant and harmless questions. Cliff answered every one to their satisfaction. *This is going to be easier than I had imagined. Perhaps the Lord will bless this event after all,* thought James. Then a thin man sitting near the end of the table, bow tie stiff and bright, suddenly cleared his throat to speak. *This is going to be trouble,* remarked James to himself. *The last man who wore a bow tie and worked for the state chewed me out for an hour.*

"Dr. Jeremiah," began the man, his voice dry and deadly serious, "if you had a teacher on your staff who eventually did not believe what the college's doctrinal statement says, what would happen to him?"

The statement hung over James like the Sword of Damocles. He knew that question was loaded. "I paused a minute, and I thought, *Jeremiah, this is your finest hour.*" James cleared his throat, sipped from the glass of water before him, and replied strongly with conviction, "Presumably, he would be fired." The thin man at the end of the table put down the papers and nodded.

"That is what ought to happen."

The North Central Association was looking for Cedarville to hold up its doctrinal statement, to be willing to stand by its beliefs. And James' answer was right on target. It was not long until the committee voted to allow Cedarville College into the North Central Association with full accreditation. This action meant that "the graduates' credits [would] be accepted for transfer to other institutions or for entrance to graduate school."[5] The final victory, the victory that James had sought so hard, the last peg in that seemingly endless row had finally been established. And the college campus went ballistic in celebration. The largest of all the mountains before him had suddenly lifted off the ground and thrown itself into the sea. And James fell to his knees and thanked God for such a time as this.

The decade of the '70s seemed to be filled with one momentous event after another. Besides traveling to Israel each year, James was speaking at more and more churches, promoting the college. The campus was expanding to fill the needs of the student body. Life was going very well. But soon James heard from his brother Edward that Flora was not doing well. Flora Jeremiah, James' mother, had been living with her son Edward and his wife, Ada, for quite some time.

After Thomas died, Flora had decided to stay in Johnson City, living by herself and trying to make out the best she could. She had established quite a number of friends, and she hated to leave. One day she hurt her ankle, and the doctor told her, 'You can't stay home alone anymore.' James found out and called Flora.

"There is a house being built in the back of where I live, and I will do my best to buy it if you come and stay with us."

"Oh, no," replied Flora, "I couldn't do that, James. I would have to leave all my friends." Eventually, however, the time came when Flora was forced to move in with someone else. She refused to travel to Cedarville, so Edward and Ada took her to the farm, "and she lost every friend she ever had." Time passed for her in isolation on the farm in Pennsylvania, and as the years whispered by, she knew she was going to die.

Ada Jeremiah took care of Flora, each day helping her dress, fixing her meals, and making sure she was comfortable. One day when Ada was putting her to bed, Flora grabbed Ada's arm and said, "Ada, one day I am going to Heaven, I am leaving, I am going to die. I don't want to, but I am not afraid." Ada consoled her, patting her gently and affectionately on the shoulder. The next morning when Ada came to dress Flora and straighten her bed, she found that Flora Jeremiah had breathed her last. She had died peacefully at the age of ninety-three.

Flora (Rozell) Jeremiah, born in 1884, entered a nation just recovering from the scars of Civil War. Her life knew hardships: a child dying at birth; Howard, her youngest dying at the age of four. She had seen the world change so much and rip itself apart through two world wars. She had grown to enjoy the pleasures and promises of a simple Christian life and had been blessed to see her sons mature and lead fulfilling lives. She had watched with a deeply felt joy her oldest assume the responsibilities of a pastor and of a college president. She had smiled with delight as his picture appeared in the local papers when he was honored with degrees. James would write years later concerning mothers in general, "Charles Dickens said that it should be somewhere written that the 'virtues of the mother shall be visited on their children as well as the sins of the father.' "[6] These virtues had enabled the son of a farmer to become a respected president of a college. And James would always remember her spirit and courage.

As 1976, the bicentennial of the United States, approached, James was thinking of his own "bicentennial" and beyond. Perhaps it was time for him to consider retirement. It was Christmas vacation, and the snow had lightly powdered the grass outside his house. He and Ruby would soon be wrapped up in the festivities of the season. The grandchildren would be coming over, or James would go to visit them, and yet a weight burdened his soul. In the quiet of his office, he picked up a pen and wrote,

> Since I know God put me here, I do not intend to change direction until He makes very clear the direction I should follow. At the same time, I sincerely desire to place the needs and the cause of Cedarville College above my own personal interests.[7]

The college was moving forward at a rapid pace, perhaps too rapidly for the aging patriarch to handle. He thought of his "four horsemen," the men who were truly running and developing the school. In just a few years, the college had doubled in size, and finances were strong; but there was still debt on the new chapel, the chapel that the board of trustees had named after him. So much was yet to be done, while so much had been accomplished. James was sixty-two years old. His bones were getting a little stiff and weaker every year. His mind was still sharp, but how long could he stay this way? He sat down to write to the board of trustees.

> My question is, How can I best help in the program of progress that lies before us? Frankly, I am not sure I can carry the heavy responsibility that would be expected of me. Nor am I sure it would be fair to the college to begin such an expansion program if I cannot carry my part of the responsibility. The prospects of all this may be greater because the load is heavier as the college grows, or because I will be 65 in about two years.[8]

However he was to leave and whenever he was to leave, he wanted to leave on good terms.

> I would like it much better if we could agree that it is *our* decision. Through the years we have enjoyed a great time of fellowship as we have worked together. I need your help and advice now as much or more than ever before. The fact that the time is moving on means sooner or later the termination of my present relationship with the college must come. The Board of Trustees must determine the best time for this change to be made.[9]

James put down the pen and mailed the letter to the board, a terrible weight now off his shoulders. The decision for resignation, removal, or replacement was now up to God. And God had never let him down.

But as the new year began, James found that his work as president was not quite over. "One pitfall in Christian education is hiring faculty who are not in sympathy with us; they are just taking it for a job." Several students had gone to James' office and expressed confusion and anger at what one professor was teaching in the Bible classes. James inquired further and discovered that the man had been professing that Jesus had a "derived deity," that Christ was not always the Son of God. So James called the man into his office.

"What you are teaching is not Scriptural."

"Oh, yes it is," retorted the professor smugly.

"Not the way we see it, brother," boomed James. "We believe it is unscriptural, and you can't teach it."

"Oh, but I have to," replied the man. James stared at him, a fire brewing just below the surface.

"You are through, brother," pronounced James suddenly. And the professor packed his bags and left the school. "That was all I could do. I couldn't do anything else, because he was violating the Word of God."

The board of trustees began searching for James' replacement. Several names were dropped or pursued, but one continually kept coming up: Paul Dixon.

Dixon was an evangelist working within the confines of the GARBC. He had a large ministry from professional athletes to local churches. He was speaking all over the country to hundreds of thousands each year. He had a master of divinity degree from Temple Seminary but had no experience in the world of academia. In fact, when Paul Dixon was approached by the board to interview for the position of president, his reply was less than enthusiastic:

> It really knocked me over! My response was, You're crazy! How in the world can you ask someone to be president of something that is going 150 miles an hour, who has never led anything?[10]

James' response to Dixon as a potential replacement was, "I thought about it, and I thought, *This guy has been preaching all over the country, and he ought to have a lot of friends. And it would be nice to tap into those friends.*" The truth of the matter was that James saw a lot of himself in the young preacher. He knew that if God was choosing this man, then no one could step in the way of it. Yes, Paul Dixon had no experience in running a college, but neither had James. At least Paul had an advanced degree from a seminary; James had not had even that. There was every reason in the world to look for someone more qualified, but there was also every reason in the world to hire him as president. James sat down with his potential replacement and had a long heart-to-heart talk:

> We [saw] things much alike, and we had for a long time before he became president. His philosophy of having a broad base for the organization to touch as many lives as you can, to try to minister to people instead of trying to restrict them, [was] exactly what I am for."[11]

That broad base James referred to was extremely important in the growth of the college and its impact. Ken St. Clair, Cliff Johnson, Richard McIntosh, Lee Turner, and others who were added to the team later laid the foundations that Paul Dixon would build upon. James would reflect,

> I could go away on a meeting—and I had to be gone a lot—and I had real heartfelt confidence that if there was a decision to be made, they would make the right one. And one of the highest honors ever paid to me was how long those men stayed with Paul Dixon after I left. And that doesn't happen very often in this realm.

James was a ferocious speaker with an arduous schedule. He would travel all over the country. "Any place I had a meeting—Ohio, Pennsylvania, New York, Iowa, and as far away as California"—Ruby would jump into the RV, and the two of them would go. This traveling placed extra strain on those at the college, but the results from James' promotional meetings were indisputable. And his traveling was one key factor in hiring a new president: James loathed to give up his traveling and speaking. But if the college were to develop further, it would need a fresh new face. And that would work in both the college's interest and in James', for the lessening of his responsibilities would allow him to do what he really enjoyed: speaking about the college, presenting the gospel, spreading the Word of God without the daily burdens of administration.

When it was decided that Paul Dixon would become the next president of Cedarville College, James was both excited and saddened by the transition. On June 4, 1977, James spoke at the commencement ceremony. His voice was steady, but neither the sorrow nor his tenacious spirit could be missed:

> The purpose of this announcement is to say that next year will be my last to serve as president of Cedarville College. . . . The Board of Trustees has unanimously voted to ask me to serve as Chancellor at the end of my tenure as president. This statement is not to be misconstrued as a resignation. I am not resigning, nor am I quitting. This is simply an announcement of what I believe will be a greater ministry of evangelism and Bible teaching for me and a means of opening new and greater opportunities for the college as we work together with the common goals of a better Cedarville College.[12]

The progress that the school had made under James' guidance was unmistakable, and as James would say, "miraculous." He had started with 100 students, and in 1978 the school had 1,250. He had begun with eight buildings on 15 acres of land, and in 1978 the campus boasted of 37 buildings spreading out over 180 acres. James had eked out a struggling annual budget of $95,000 when he took office, but he was leaving behind an annual budget of $4.5 million, from total assets of $325,000, to assets of $9.7 million. These accomplishments were indeed the hand of God moving and using a man with such humble beginnings. James was asked to take the next step, and he did, reluctantly but in obedience. And God moved him beyond all that he could have ever hoped or imagined.

The next year, his final year as president, James continued his blustery schedule of speaking engagements, daily radio ministry, and visiting his sons and daughters. It was then that he paid a visit to his brother Edward and his sister-in-law Ada. Edward had "a house in Johnson City and worked there for a while. And his wife's people had a farm. They inherited it." The farm was located in Pennsylvania, and soon Edward found himself running it, growing crops, living off the land. It was a good place to live—quiet, peaceful, away from the bustle of the world. Edward had changed after World War II. Like most veterans of war, he had a hard time adjusting and relating to people on an everyday level. The war and its horrors had taken its toll. A crust had formed around his heart, and he isolated himself from the pain. "He loved his cows. He said once, 'I can talk to cows, and they don't talk back; people, I don't know what to do with.' "

In a sense, Edward had become a lot like Thomas, his father. Years later James remarked, "I have always maintained a relationship with Edward. (He doesn't maintain one with me.) And I'm going to do that as long as I can. I go to see him and will continue to do that. I have been here for forty-five years, and he has never come to visit." Edward was the type of man who stayed to himself, who desired nothing back from the world. And life around him rolled on.

When the 1978–79 academic year approached, James handed over the mantle of the college to Paul Dixon with no strings attached. This transition exemplified James' godly character and demonstrated the spirit of a man completely devoted to his God. When such a power shift takes place, whether in Christian circles or outside, certain things often take place. Scars occur, along with rifts in the program and, at times, deep lasting wounds that shatter the institution or affect people in every strata. And this effect is truer in the world of academics than in any other sphere. A college president is in such a powerful, prestigious position that when a change of command occurs, dissention and even resignations soon follow.

But that was not what happened at Cedarville College. Indeed, as commented earlier, the "four horsemen" stayed on, and even, in some sense, so did James. And this should not be surprising. From his early days on, James' life was God using an obedient man, not a man using God to further his own agenda. In fact, James embraced his new role as chancellor to relieve himself of the burden of the college and to pursue his speaking. This he did with a vengeance, for during his first year as chancellor,

> [James] held 31 conferences and ministered in two seminaries and three mission fields. In all, he preached 208 messages. As he traveled around the world, he sought to meet alumni on an individual or group basis.[13]

The road ahead of James and Ruby was bright and exciting. They had weathered so many storms together, always supporting one another hand in hand, their eyes focused on God. It had been such a wonderful ride, and now they took that next step into the twilight of their lives. And though the pace of their lives did not slow down, the physical obstacles became increasingly hard to topple. Soon James would be faced with the most terrible mountain of his life, terrible because its cliffs were steep, its edges unforgiving, its path lonely and dark. And this time he would have no company to bear the burden, for down this road Ruby could not travel.

ENDNOTES

1. Cedarville, Ohio. Cedarville College. "Christian Sojourn to Europe and the Bible Lands." Letter. 31 July 1969.
2. Ibid.
3. All quotations of James T. Jeremiah, unless otherwise noted, are taken from interviews conducted by the author.

4. J. Murray Murdoch, *Cedarville College: A Century of Commitment* (Cedarville, Ohio: Cedarville College, 1987), 137.

5. *Xenia Gazette,* 14 April 1975.

6. James T. Jeremiah, *The House That Stands* (Cedarville, Ohio: Christian Educational Publications, 1974), 22.

7. Murdoch, 142.

8. Ibid., 143.

9. Ibid.

10. Ibid., 148.

11. Ibid., 150.

12. Ibid., 144.

13. Ibid., 151, 152.

Chapter 7

Such a Legacy
(1980–present)

"We had a bus once...." The year was 1980, and James was presenting a message titled *Cedarville College: Past, Present, and Future*. "... And we used to take the choir all over the place. And one thing about this bus you could count on—it wouldn't run.... It got so bad that they used to call it 'the lamentations of Jeremiah.'"[1] The audience—which was comprised of friends, faculty, and the entire student body—applauded with delight. James was fulfilling his role as chancellor of the college in the most effective way he knew how: tell the story. He closed his message by saying,

> It all comes back to this: we must have gift income in step with student enrollment. We must keep at it constantly, telling the story, praying.... And keep in mind that the past of this institution is nothing if it does not have a good future, and if it does not keep pressing on in the future, and working for better things in the future. May God help us in this time of great opportunity to meet the challenge.[2]

The 1980s and 1990s, more than any other time span, demonstrate the breadth of the technological and social changes that James Jeremiah witnessed during his lifetime. From 1914, the year of James' birth—when telephones were just coming into use, when automobiles were thought to be a fad, when horses and buggies were the only tried and proven method of transportation—from that year up through the 1990s, the growth in technology is awe inspiring. James and his generation witnessed the household telephone, the advent of the television, spaceships to the moon, and in the 1980s the introduction of the home computer. The media outlets alone have so drastically changed during James' lifetime that, to this present generation, the first media outlets appear archaic and quite simplistic. James' father had gathered his news through word of mouth and the local newspaper. James gathered his news from the newspapers and radio. Soon the radio was largely replaced by the television, and the television expanded by cable, then satellite, and eventually the Internet. From a delay of nearly a day, the news outlets have become instantaneous. And James Jeremiah had not only witnessed but actively engaged in most of these changes.

James' mother, Flora, washed her clothes in a washbasin with a ringer. Ruby saw the creation of the washing machine as a household appliance. The daily materials and goods that we take for granted were almost nonexistent in Flora Jeremiah's day; but by the time James and Ruby were raising their family, they had already begun to weave themselves into the culture of society. It is important to drive home this point; that is, the rapid transformation of this society and culture. For it is then that James' life becomes a mirror, a special artifact, a narrative of someone who has seen and participated in the cultural, technological, and moral revolutions that spanned nearly a century of furious and at times nihilistic advancement.

In the 1980s James and Ruby were traveling all over the country, speaking in churches and at the GARBC annual conferences, to young people and old, all the while spreading the gospel and publicizing Cedarville College. They spent their time visiting their children and grandchildren as well. David and Maryalce lived in California. David and his radio ministry were becoming a household name; Maryalyce had earned a Ph.D. and was working at the University of California at Fullerton. Loisanne lived in Tennessee, her husband involved with radio; and young Jim, having graduated from Cedarville, was also out in the world of ministry. It would seem that such retirement would afford James and Ruby a long-deserved respite from the daily grind of the college. But James became restless, for he did not like to lie about and do nothing. He was still a dynamo of energy and filled with two objectives, two passions, that consumed all of his heart and mind: evangelize the lost and promote the college! Cedarville College had taken off. Under the new direction of Paul Dixon and his strategic planning, its enrollment was controlled, new money was acquired from various sources outside the GARBC churches, and faculty and students were pushed up to the next level of excellence. James would never have to worry again about the financial and academic future of the college. The mantle had been passed and now rested on firm and committed shoulders.

One day James and Ruby traveled back to Johnson City to visit his parents' graves. "When I got there, the plots were covered with brush."[3] The small cemetery had not been kept up. James tried to pull out as much vegetation as he could, but the job was too much, the plot and stones too far gone. "It bothered me that there had been no maintenance." He would go back year after year to attend to those matters and see that something was done.

James had become a household name to many of the members of GARBC churches across the state and to other Christians as well; for his radio broadcast *Light for Living* had been out in the airwaves for many years. Much like his son David, James had utilized the medium of radio to broadcast a daily message of hope, inspiration, and challenge to as many souls as he could. His daily message was powerful and filled with anecdotes and examples:

> Annie Johnson Flint wrote these encouraging lines about the God Who does the impossible: "I cannot, but God can. / Oh balm for all my cares! / The burden that I drop / His hand will lift and bear; / Though eagle pinions tire, / I walk where once I ran. / This is my strength, to know / I cannot, but God can."[4]

This message titled "Things Impossible" broadcast on Tuesday, November 22, 1983, and ended with these words:

> Say, friend, one impossible thing He can do is save you. You cannot do that for yourself. Submit to the Savior now and be saved forever. With Him, all things are possible.[5]

But soon the radio ministry became burdensome and his traveling schedule more demanding than James had anticipated. As a result, he decided to terminate the broadcast in 1985. Beginning with his early days in Toledo in the 1940s, James had been sharing his Biblical insights—his messages of hope and repentance—to hundreds of thousands; his radio ministry spanned more than forty years. It had thrived at every location God had called James to, and now this part of his legacy and sermons would end. But James' vocabulary contained no such word as "finished," and by the early 1990s, he would be engaged in a new mission, another radio ministry called *Senior Advantage*.

During these days the accomplishments of James Jeremiah, his commitment to the college, and his lasting legacy to the city of Cedarville and even the surrounding city of Dayton were being eulogized. A large Dayton paper proclaimed in a Sunday supplement headline: "The Reverend Who Saved Cedarville."[6] This article once again told the story of James, of Cedarville College, and of a God Who uses men for His glory. The author, Tim Fish, proclaimed, "In a period of hard times for schools of its size, Cedarville is one of the few in the country that continues to grow.

Cedarville College is a legacy with which Jeremiah can be proud. Of course, Jeremiah's life is such a legacy."[7] The article is truly a great piece, and it truly vindicates the man and the institution that were somewhat denigrated in the same paper during the previous three decades.

In 1985 James and Ruby decided that they would move to California to be closer to their children and their grandchildren. It was a time of rejoicing, a time of leaving behind and starting afresh, a time to enjoy the fruits of what God had done in both their lives. The two packed up, traveled across the country, and found themselves in a small house in California. The climate was much more agreeable to both of them. The cold, damp winters in Cedarville had penetrated deep into their bones. Both James and Ruby were in their seventies, and anything that could be done to prevent the creaks and annoying pains was worthy of effort.

It was in California, after the couple had finally settled in, that James began to see a very disturbing sign in Ruby. Even before the move, Ruby was forgetting things and could not remember the names of good friends. *A change will do her good*, thought James. *Get her away from the winters, allow her to be with her children and grandchildren.* Soon it was apparent, however, that Ruby was far worse than anyone had at first thought. She was exhibiting more severe symptoms: forgetting where she was, at times mumbling to herself, and acting as though she were lost in some other world. And yet, at other times, she was as lucid as ever. James decided that it would be best for them to move back to Cedarville and into a familiar place with familiar people. "I knew that she wasn't well." Their stay in California was short-lived, and the most painful moments of James' life were about to begin.

James would recall later, "I noticed one day, when I went into the bedroom, that she was trying to get dressed, and she had her clothes on in the most absurd way you could imagine." Ruby was exhibiting all the signs of Alzheimer's disease:

> Alzheimer's is a degenerative disease that usually begins gradually, causing a person to forget recent events or familiar tasks. How rapidly it advances varies from person to person, but the brain disease eventually causes confusion, personality and behavior changes, and impaired judgment. Communication becomes difficult as the affected person struggles to find words, finish thoughts, or follow directions. Eventually, most people with Alzheimer's become unable to care for themselves.[8]

Ruby was persistently challenged by buttons and small tasks; she would wear several shirts, mistake underclothes for hats, and place keys in the freezer.[9] "She couldn't think," remembered James. "I can't explain it. It's just an awful thing."

James was just as busy as always: going to churches and to the college, attending chapel services, speaking with the students; and it became clear that he would not be able to attend to Ruby's increasing needs.

> Four kids and three doctors told me that I would have to put her in a home because I couldn't take care of her. There was nothing I could do. . . . I didn't know what to do with someone like that.

Meanwhile, Ruby was falling deeper and deeper into her own world.

Yet sometimes she would astound people:

> David and I took her to lunch one day, and I said, "Ruby, I want you to pray." And when she was through, David looked at me and responded, "I don't believe it. Man-oh-man, I don't believe it." She had prayed just like she had always prayed.

Having made the decision to place Ruby in a home,

Such a Legacy

James—filled with inexpressible anguish, a pulling and clawing on his insides—took Ruby to a doctor so that she could be admitted to the home.

> I took her to the doctor. She was in the hospital two or three days, and then she went to that place. She never complained. And they took good care of her.

What anxiety, what complete despair James must have felt as he left the parking lot that day. Here his helpmate, his companion who had seen him through all the tough times—those days when there was no money, when it looked like the church and its pastor were through, when she alone printed the college brochures in the basement of a building on campus—was now somewhere down a road where James could not follow. He could only watch and pray:

> There is nothing beyond the reach of prayer except that which lies beyond the will of God.... One reason we fail in our Christian lives is our failure to ask of God. The promise to answer should encourage us to ask.[10]

The power of their lives together, the force of their determination when all the odds for success were against them—all of this had driven James closer to Ruby and to obedience to God.

James visited Ruby every day. He would spend as much time as he could with her and then go off to those meetings or engagements that packed his life. Every Sunday he would pick her up and take her to church, "and she would sit there and listen to the pastor preach, and you would think that she was as normal as she could be." On beautiful spring days, James would pick up Ruby, and the two of them would go off together to have a picnic. By this time she was far gone, her mind wheeling and spinning, fragmenting into shards of reality and imagination. But they would sit and watch the trees blowing and listen to the birds or the children in the park laughing and playing. A terrible feeling of despair still clawed at James' insides. He knew that the greatest human gift God had ever given him was slowly and incrementally stepping toward her appointed final place with her Lord, and with each step, moving farther and farther away from him.

James was living in a house that the college had bought for Ruby and him upon their return to Cedarville. But now it seemed empty. Every night before going to bed, he would pray that Ruby would be taken care of and that God would grant him the grace he needed to face the inevitable. "It was so hard. . . . I would go down to the home, and she would be wandering around aimlessly." This was one of the lowest moments in James Jeremiah's life, for before his eyes the precious life of his wife was withering away:

> One day, I went to get her for a picnic. I drove into the place and saw an ambulance. I went inside, and when I came into the hallway, I saw a stretcher. Well, on the stretcher lay Ruby.

Ruby had gotten a sore on her foot, and the doctors had given her medicine to treat the infection. Then, quite suddenly, she had had a stroke. "She died that day. I went to the hospital, but they would not allow me to see her." Fortunately for her, Ruby did not suffer long. The people who hurt were her family.

Ruby Lathrop Jeremiah, who had been born one year after James, thus died in 1991. Her memorial service was held at Grace Baptist Church in Cedarville, the church she and James had attended together for thirty years. The board of trustees and all the church family and friends, along with James' children, gathered around her grave and celebrated her life.

Later James received a plaque in honor of Ruby. The inscription reads:

Honorary Alumna of the Year 1993
Awarded to
RUBY LATHROP JEREMIAH
1915–1991
In Recognition of Her Outstanding Contributions
To Cedarville College
Presented to
Dr. James T. Jeremiah
From the
Cedarville College Alumni Association

The most godly woman James had ever known, the most caring and obedient to the Word of God, had suddenly been taken from him.

> The housewife is a very important person in the family equation. With her patience and love, she brings differing individuals to mutual understanding; she transforms a house into a home; often she is the one with Christian common sense who keeps the family happy and God-glorifying. Carefully read Proverbs 31 and observe that of the godly housewife it is said: "The heart of her husband doth safely trust in her. . . . [H]er children rise up and call her blessed."[11]

James felt a sudden tearing of his heart, a sudden weight upon his shoulders that he thought he could not bear alone. But this weight was lessened by clinging to the hope that Ruby was in a better place.

> For the child of God, Heaven will be an eternal vacation, not from service, but from the troubles that plague our mortal bodies. "The dead who die in the Lord . . . shall rest from their labors, and their works do follow them. . . . There shall be no more death, nor sorrow, nor crying; and there shall be no more pain, for the former things have passed away" (Revelation 14:13; 21:4). In the presence of

> Christ in Heaven, the child of God shall rest
> from his physical suffering and the many other
> burdens we carry on earth. "Just think of
> stepping on shore, and finding it Heaven," of
> waking up and finding it "Home"—a place
> where we shall rest from all that has troubled,
> burdened, or wearied us.[12]

But now James had to face an empty home, night after night of silence, save for the chortling whispers of the enemy bidding him to despair. And his heart was indeed shattered in a million pieces. Earlier, in 1984, James had given a series of messages about Heaven. Those messages, one in particular, suddenly resonated with a world of meaning:

> Heaven is as real, and much more lasting, than
> any city on earth. Heaven is a real place, much
> more than the "beautiful isle of somewhere"
> described by the poet. . . . To be sure, the child
> of God will be satisfied in Heaven, that place
> Christ has gone to prepare, but we can now
> enjoy Heaven on earth if we will trust and
> obey Christ today.[13]

Ruby Jeremiah had slipped away from the land of the living and was safe from the barbs and arrows of this world. It was up to James to pull himself out of the depression he found himself in. The road before him seemed to stretch out bleak and ominous into an eternity of darkness, and God was once again calling for him to trust and obey—to dare to move the mountain!

The 1990s continued on, and James tried to busy himself with the daily routine of the college and of speaking. He was still lonely, but a fire was beginning to burn again. "However you view the Christian life, it requires determination as well as faith," James proclaimed behind the microphone at WCDR on his new program, *Senior Advantage:*

> A farmer had a horse that was blind and old.
> One day [the horse] fell into an old well. Since

> the horse and the well were useless to him, the farmer decided to fill up the well and leave the horse buried in it. He shoveled the dirt into the well, but the horse was not ready to be buried. When the dirt fell on him, he shook it off and kept beating it under his feet. Gradually the well filled up, and the horse rose higher and higher until he was able to step out and gallop to the pasture. The moral? There is no need for you to be buried under troubles, discouragement, and hard times unless you are willing to be. Shake off your disappointments. Look to the Lord and keep treading. You will rise above your circumstances and go on to a new life of victory![14]

God was likewise not yet through with His servant James, for He was calling James once more to the breach.

> Select whatever metaphor you choose—journey, battle, pilgrimage, or warfare—the goals are the same. If life is a journey, it must be completed. If life is a battle, it must be won. If life is a pilgrimage, it must be concluded. If it is a race, it must be run and completed.[15]

James was now seventy-seven years old and still in good health, except for some minor aches and pains. His muscles had deteriorated as those of any other seventy-seven-year-old; his waist was no longer as thin as it had been when he was sixty. But he had breath, and he still had a mission: evangelize the lost and promote Cedarville College. And that is exactly what he did.

God demands our obedience; but obeying is hard, and the flesh is weak. The first step toward healing is to know that when you take that step, God will not allow you to be crushed, to be consumed by the terrible voices and emotions that wish to convey you to the abyss of despair. It was no different with Abraham. God did not call him to sacrifice Isaac in the beginning. No, God had proved over and over again how unfailing and incomprehensible His love for

Abraham truly was. And this could be said for James as well. God had shown him over and over again that all he need do is trust and obey. Each time the stakes were higher; each new test, the foothold farther and farther away. But with each act of obedience, James realized that though he could not see the foothold, it was there; for God had promised that it would be. From the faithless man's perspective, James was leaping to places that seemed ludicrous and reckless. But to the faithful man, the steps that seemed to bridge great chasms were in reality only baby steps. His body was slowly decaying—the way of all flesh—but as long as his spirit and mind could be used by God, he would keep taking steps of obedience.

In 1972, when his radio ministry was not *Light for Living* but *Campus Challenge,* James considered the problem of old age. Though comparatively he was a spring chicken (fifty-eight years old), his words resonate with a prophetic voice:

> It is true that everyone of us, so far as our bodies are concerned, will be conquered by old age, if death does not take us or the Lord does not return before we reach the "threescore years and ten." A better way to face the future, however, is to know that at any time we have a God Who has delivered us and will carry us through the trials of our years and the years of our trial.[16]

And as the years began to pass—at first slowly, painfully, each new day, and at times each new hour—James filled his life with living in the land of the living, with the joy of his salvation. In time his mission and obedience consumed the torment of Ruby's death. When asked years later how he had endured the time, he answered, "I traveled sometimes, but I knew I had a job to do." Little did he know that another joy was to enter his life, a gift from God specifically designed for him from the beginning of time.

In 1993, Cliff Johnson and Ken St. Clair were pushing James to ask someone out to the college's Junior-Senior Banquet. They had witnessed James' recovery, understood that he had decided to move forward; and they wanted him to make his decision public. James already had someone in mind to take to the banquet; for, unbeknown to Cliff and Ken, he had been taking Ethel Rayburn out to dinner for quite some time. Ethel had been good friends with Ruby and had lived in Cedarville since 1971.

Ethel and her husband, Marlin, had been missionaries in Kentucky, and then God called them to Wheaton College. Marlin later became a pastor in Flint, Michigan, and in Iowa. After several years of moving around to various places, Ethel and Marlin moved to Cedarville, where Ethel took a job as a secretary in the college library. She held that position for sixteen years, while her husband worked in the Speech Department. In 1989, Marlin was diagnosed with cancer. He died two years later, so Ethel went through the same grieving process as James, and at about the same time. When asked how long Ethel and Marlin had been married, Ethel responded, "Almost fifty years: forty-nine years, ten months and two weeks."[17] The extent of her loss was obviously as devastating as James'. While Ruby was edging toward death, Marlin was as well. In a very real sense James and Ethel were partakers in each other's pain and bereavement. It just so happened that Ethel was on vacation when Ruby died.

In July 1992, James asked Ethel if she wished to have dinner with him. She agreed, and they enjoyed a nice quiet evening. "It was every once in a while" when those occasions happened, when both were feeling down or one needed a boost. But they were always out of the public's eye.[18] And then came the 1993 Junior-Senior Banquet. James asked Ethel to attend the banquet with him, and they were accompanied by Ken and Ida St. Clair. This was Ethel and

James' first appearance among all their friends. The evening was a great success.

Then on January 8, 1994, James showed up on Ethel's doorstep. Ethel was planning to go to Florida for a three-month vacation, and James knew that he had to act quickly. He stood in front of her and proclaimed, "I want you to have a ring before you go to Florida."[19] And as far as the time element was concerned, his idea was simple: "You can't stay for three months!" So the last week in February he went down to get her and stayed in Florida for a week; afterward the two of them drove home together.[20]

On Monday, March 24, 1994, James Jeremiah took a new bride. Ethel would recall, "It was on a Monday, because that was the only time David could come. I've never heard of a Monday marriage before."[21] The wedding was held at Grace Baptist Church in Cedarville. Ethel's daughter stood up for her, and James' son Jim was the best man. His other son, David, married them, and among the distinguished family and friends was Cedarville College's president, Paul Dixon. The honeymoon couple spent time in California, and on their arrival back to Cedarville they decided to move into Ethel's existing house for logistical reasons. And as Ethel reflected much later, "That merging business [moving all their belongings] is for the birds."[22]

The breath of new life that Ethel breathed into James was remarkable. For all his years under the bridge, all the experiences stratified layer upon layer, James was still a man who needed a helpmate, someone with whom he could share his world. And James and Ethel were very much established, their personalities, daily routines, and little quirks forged in stone. But their lives moved forward. James had spent most of his winters in California or Florida—most of that time traveling across the state visiting churches, continuously telling and retelling the Cedarville College story. Several times during the 1990s, James stood before the college family and recounted the story, but more and more that tale was being told by others, and his mind was remembering only those moments that had etched their emotions into his conscience. His days filled with the mundane, and very soon he had worn a constant, smooth groove into yet another decade of the twentieth century.

"He encouraged me that every mistake in ministry is excusable except inactivity and the refusal to take risks. . . ."[23] The speaker was Dr. Tom Younger. The day was May 28, 1998, and James was being honored before the entire Cedarville College family. In 1951, Tom Younger was just a twenty-three-year-old pastor whom James had asked to take the small church in Arcanum, Ohio. Back in those days, Tom would spend hours on end at the Jeremiah home, seeking guidance and encouragement. He went on to become chairman of the board of trustees at Cedarville College and a longtime friend to James and Ruby. Tom ended his speech with a humorous but telling comment: "He truly was a man of mercy, . . . but you never wanted to mess with him. . . . I never did, but I saw what happened to those who did."[24]

James had been shocked to find out that the day's chapel was specifically and wholly devoted to him. The lights suddenly had gone out, and on the giant screen—before thousands of people—a video portrayed an amalgamation of early photographs, interviews with friends and faculty, and stirring music. Loisanne and David, his older two children, were able to attend the celebration; and halfway through, they came out from behind a closed door to surprise him. The audience exploded with applause as the obviously stunned and aging man was hugged by his son and daughter, friends, and confidants.

The years had worn on James, his face rounded and wrinkled, his large, thick bifocals gleaming in the bright light of the auditorium. Yet the fire and tenacity that had marked all of his life shone from every ounce of his being. Ethel sat beside him, a walker in front of her seat; she was to have hip surgery just a few months later.

After Tom Younger left the podium, the president of the college, Dr. Paul Dixon, took his place and bid James to come and sit on the stage. "All of us who know Dr. Jeremiah know that he is an early riser. . . . He gets up so early . . . and eventually finds his way to Bob Evans Restaurant. . . ."[25] And at that moment the vice president of food products at Bob Evans came to the podium.

> On behalf of Bob Evans, I am here to express my gratitude for the investment you have placed in us during your forty-five years of service. Although nobody has counted the number of meals that you have enjoyed at our restaurants, friends and family would estimate that it is in the thousands . . . if not tens of thousands. . . . And some days it was said that it wasn't just one meal that we served you . . . but two or three. . . .[26]

The audience erupted again—and again with cheers and applause—for it was well known that James made it a daily ritual to frequent certain places to eat and to enjoy good fellowship. The vice president continued,

> You are always quick to seek us out, no matter where your travels take you. I understand your only regret with your Holy Land tours was there was not a Bob Evans in Jerusalem. But if we ever open one there, . . . you will be first on our list to receive a grand opening invitation.[27]

And then after applause and laughter, James was presented with a mountain of gift certificates and a deed for a square foot of Bob Evans land.

A young man representing the student body then took the stage and gave James a New King James Version Thomas Nelson Study Bible. The inscription on the flyleaf read,

Such a Legacy

> To Dr. James T. Jeremiah,
> a friend and a man who loves God and served Him well.
> May God give you many more years.
> In His service,
> Sam Moore, President
> of Thomas Nelson Publishing[28]

Sam Moore was a personal friend of James, for earlier in his ministry James had sat on one of the committees that helped to revise and update the New King James edition.

Finally David Jeremiah, a nationally known radio preacher and pastor of a large church in California, rose from his seat and addressed the thousands who had gathered to honor his father. "I didn't realize this was going to be as emotional as this has been. . . ." David, now gray like his father, stood before the crowd, his voice deep and booming and filled with the love that had always bound the Jeremiah family with bands of steel:

> All of us in our own right have learned from the lessons that were drilled into us in the early days. It is overwhelming to me now when I see the evidence of God's blessing—the incredible buildings, the beautiful campus, the multitude of students. When I come here, I always remember what it was when it began, the first year I was here. The joke in our family was, "If we hadn't had a garden that summer, we all would have starved." The only thing my mother knew how to grow was squash, and I can't stand it to this day. . . .[29]

And then the tall, white-haired son cleared his throat and took on a serious tone: "I thought that my tribute to my father today should be couched in the lessons that I learned. . . ." David's voice suddenly cracked from the tremendous well of emotion forcing its way into his mind, ". . . learned growing up in this family." He remembered the days of nothing, of seeing his father and mother completely consume themselves with the college, with each other, and with the God they served:

> Ministry, in a large part, is about courage. It's easy to just minister, but it takes courage to have ministry. It took a great deal of courage to do what was done here in the early days. I remember some of the challenges, some of the discussions . . . when courage was on the line, to do the right thing, even though you knew that some folks were not going to be happy about it. Tom Younger is right: he's a merciful man, but he's nobody to mess with. He's right, nobody can move him. And I have learned from that.
>
> And you got to have faith. You know, faith is seeing those things which are not, as if they were. I don't imagine that my father saw this, in the beginning, in color; but I can promise you that he saw something like this in his head. I learned a long time ago that it is big in your head before it will be big on the corner. . . . You see it in your heart before you see it in the ground. And my father's vision for this college was very vivid in those early days. And I learned that from my father: he taught me faith . . . and tenacity.
>
> I am happy on behalf of our family to join in this tribute for my father who for forty-five years has loved this school and loved its people. . . . This is where his heart is, and this is what he started in 1953 when we moved here. And I know how much he loves all of you and how much he loves this place. So, Dad, I salute you, and I salute Paul Dixon for making him an honored man in this place.[30]

The crowd erupted with applause as David walked over to James and embraced him, tears in both men's eyes apparent. James was presented with a memory box containing hundreds of letters written by friends, faculty, and loved ones. And as the hour wound down, Dr. Dixon pronounced that the board had decided to provide a three-month stay at a condominium of James and Ethel's choice located in California so that they could visit their children. And finally a painting was bestowed upon him, a collage of images and scenes set around the painted portrait of James.

James, very much moved by this display of affection, took to the podium in response to the overwhelming applause:

> I really don't deserve all that. One of the things that thrills me as I look over this school is that what was done was accomplished by God alone. God is with us and has been, has given us many good friends, good times, and many graduates who are going out to serve the Lord. I want to thank you all. I don't have the words I want to say, but I do want to say thank you.[31]

James walked down from the podium and over to his seat. After the special chapel ended, he and his family made their way to a banquet in honor of his forty-five years of service to the Lord.

It is awesome to reflect on the course that God set for the son of a farmer in 1914, how He swept him into His kingdom and bid him serve Him, no matter what. The steps of obedience that are so obvious in his life humble the most ardent man of faith. When God called James to be faithful, he was; when He called him to be dogmatic, he was; when He called him to serve at any cost, James did.

In the twilight of this millennium, in the age of prosperity and cynicism, James T. Jeremiah stands as a benchmark to all, a reminder and encouragement to any willing person of what is possible, what can be achieved if one has faith and a personal relationship with the God of the universe. James T. Jeremiah took to heart with all of his soul the Lord's words to his disciples in Matthew 21:21 and 22:

> Verily I say unto you, If ye have faith, and doubt not, ye shall not only do this which is

> done to the fig tree, but also if ye shall say
> unto this mountain, Be thou removed, and be
> thou cast into the sea; it shall be done. And all
> things, whatsoever ye shall ask in prayer,
> believing, ye shall receive.

May we dare to put these words into practice in our own lives as we walk humbly and mightily with our God.

ENDNOTES

1. James T. Jeremiah, "Cedarville College: Past, Present and Future," Cedarville College, Cedarville, Ohio, 1980, speech.
2. Ibid.
3. All quotations of James T. Jeremiah, unless otherwise noted, are taken from interviews conducted by the author.
4. James T. Jeremiah, "Things Impossible." *Light for Living*. WCDR, Cedarville, Ohio. 22 November 1983.
5. Ibid.
6. Tim Fish, "The Reverend Who Saved Cedarville," *Dayton Daily News*, 8 December 1985.
7. Ibid., 20.
8. The Alzheimer's Association. Internet. http://www.alz.org/facts/rtwhatis.htm.
9. These are general characteristics of patients with Alzheimer's disease.
10. James T. Jeremiah, "Why Pray." *Light for Living*. WCDR, Cedarville, Ohio. 25 July 1983.
11. James T. Jeremiah, *God's Answers to Our Anxieties* (Grand Rapids: Baker Book House, 1978), 40.
12. James T. Jeremiah, "Heaven on Earth VI: Rest." *Light for Living*. WCDR, Cedarville, Ohio. 24 September 1984.
13. James T. Jeremiah, "Heaven on Earth III: Satisfaction." *Light for Living*. WCDR, Cedarville, Ohio. 19 September 1984.
14. James T. Jeremiah, "Keep On Going." *Light for Living*. WCDR, Cedarville, Ohio. 16 September 1983.
15. Ibid.
16. James T. Jeremiah, "Facing Old Age." *Campus Challenge*. WCDR, Cedarville, Ohio. 1 September 1972.
17. Ethel Jeremiah, personal interview, 11 September 1998. The previous information about Ethel and James came from this interview with Ethel.
18. Ibid.

Such a Legacy

19. Ibid.
20. Ibid.
21. Ibid.
22. Ibid.
23. *Dr. Jeremiah Tribute.* Cedarville College, 28 May 1998, videocassette.
24. Ibid.
25. Ibid.
26. Ibid.
27. Ibid.
28. Ibid.
29. Ibid.
30. Ibid.
31. Ibid.